JUMBO
BIBLE
Winter
WORD GAMES

T0015711

JUMBO
BIBLE
Winter
WORD GAMES

BARBOUR
kidz

© 2023 by Barbour Publishing, Inc.

ISBN 978-1-63609-664-3

Scripture quotations marked sᴋᴊᴠ are taken from the Barbour Simplified KJV, copyright © 2022, by Barbour Publishing, Inc., Uhrichsville, Ohio 44683. All rights reserved.

Scripture quotations marked ɴʟᴠ are taken from the New Life Version copyright © 1969 and 2003 by Barbour Publishing, Inc., Uhrichsville, Ohio, 44683. All rights reserved.

Scripture quotations marked ᴋᴊᴠ are taken from the King James Version of the Bible.

Published by Barbour Publishing, Inc., 1810 Barbour Drive, Uhrichsville, Ohio 44683, www.barbourbooks.com

Our mission is to inspire the world with the life-changing message of the Bible.

ecpa Member of the
Evangelical Christian
Publishers Association

Printed in the United States of America.

001751 0823 BP

JUMBO BIBLE Winter woRd GAMeS...

great for bad weather days, long cold nights, or any "I'm bored" moments!

Perfect for kids ages 8 to 12, this book is jam-packed with Bible-based pencil-and-paper games to challenge and amuse, entertain and educate. Inside you'll find the following types of puzzles:

- **Crosswords**: Fill in the puzzle grid by answering the "across" and "down" clues. If you need help, verse references are provided.

- **Word searches**: In the puzzle grid, find and circle the **bold** search words in the scripture—the words might run forward, backward, up, down, or diagonally. If the <u>search words</u> are underlined, they will appear together in the puzzle grid.

- **Decoders**: For every two-digit number in the puzzle, find the correct letter in the decoder grid. The first number refers to the row (the numbers running down the left side of the grid). The second number indicates the column (the numbers running across the top of the grid). After you've determined all the letters and placed them in the puzzle, they'll spell out an important verse.

- **Acrostics**: Read the definition in the left-hand column and write the word it describes in the right-hand column. Then place the coded letters from the right-hand column into the puzzle below to spell out a Bible verse.

- **Spotty Headlines**: Fill in the missing letters of each "head-line," which relates to a Bible character, thing, or story. Then unscramble those letters to form a name or word, the subject of the headline.

- **Scrambles**: Also called "anagrams," these are funny words and phrases that contain the scrambled letters of a Bible word or name. Unscramble the letters to figure out the right answer! (We've given some clues to help you.)

- **Bible Diamonds**: This new puzzle challenges you to answer the clues by spelling out words in the diamond grid. Start in the center box and then move one square at a time, in any direction, until you find the answer. You may even double back to letters in the diamond! To help you out, we've provided the first letters of some answers.

Looking for something fun to do? Sharpen your pencil and tackle *Jumbo Bible Winter Word Games*!

CLUES

The Son of God (Mark 1:1): J ____ ____ ____ ____

To look for (Matthew 6:33): ____ ____ ____ ____

Saul, David, or Solomon, for example (1 Samuel 18:6;
   2 Samuel 5:3; 1 Kings 4:1): K ____ ____ ____

A LION IN THE SNOW

Benaiah was the son of Jehoiada, the **son** of a **valiant** man from **Kabzeel**, who had done **many acts**. He **slew** two **lionlike** men of **Moab**. He also <u>went down</u> and slew a lion in the **middle** of a **pit** on a **snowy** day.

2 SAMUEL 23:20 SKJV

SPOTTY HEADLINE

●ON OF GOD
●O●RNEY● TO ●GYPT

Hint: He went as a baby.

___ ___ ___ ___ ___

```
B  T  H  C  E  L  D  D  I  M
L  V  A  L  I  A  N  T  F  E
E  M  I  A  N  D  J  T  K  L
E  N  A  C  F  R  V  I  I  F
Z  K  N  T  M  N  L  M  V  P
B  S  E  S  O  N  M  M  J  L
A  N  B  S  O  S  B  A  O  M
K  O  M  I  L  L  V  B  N  K
V  W  L  E  K  L  Q  Y  B  Y
K  Y  W  E  N  T  D  O  W  N
```

GIVING GIFTS

Across

2. Has a shape but weighs nothing (James 1:17)

6. Not having much money (Matthew 19:21)

8. The hand fewer people use (Matthew 6:3)

9. All shook up (Luke 6:38)

Down

1. Not strong (Acts 20:35)

3. Wanting to do something; not reluctant (2 Corinthians 8:12)

4. Found below a tree (1 Timothy 6:10 KJV)

5. Capable (Deuteronomy 16:17)

7. Lots of money (Proverbs 3:9 NLV)

THE STORY OF JONAH

JONAH 2:10 NLV

Jonah found himself in the belly of a fish after disobeying God. Crack the code to find out what happened next!

_____ ran from God (Jonah 1:3).   8-7-32-20-33

The _____ became afraid
when the storm hit (Jonah 1:5).   25-36-28-29-35-15-24

The storm _____ when Jonah
was thrown overboard (Jonah 1:15).   12-10-14-3-31-9-6

Nineveh had _____ days to
repent (Jonah 3:4).   23-19-22-34-1

Jonah made a _____ outside of
Nineveh (Jonah 4:5 KJV).   39-38-4-18-30

A plant protected Jonah
from the _____ (Jonah 4:6).   2-11-27

To leave behind (Jonah 2:8 KJV)   17-26-13-16-21-5-37

34-30-9-32   10-33-37   29-26-22-6   16-3-4-5-9   18-19

34-30-37   17-28-12-33,   36-32-6   28-34   2-31-28-10

8-14-27-36-30   4-11-34   38-27-18-26   10-30-37   6-22-1

29-21-32-6.

	1	2	3	4	5
1	H	U	V	Y	M
2	D	F	B	L	N
3	X	T	J	G	K
4	A	S	C	E	R
5	Q	W	O	I	P

GENESIS 1:31 SKJV

41-25-21   34-53-21   42-41-52   44-13-44-45-14-32-11-54-25-34

32-11-41-32   11-44   11-41-21   15-41-21-44,   41-25-21

23-44-11-53-24-21,   54-32   52-41-42   13-44-45-14

34-53-53-21.   41-25-21   32-11-44   44-13-44-25-54-25-34

41-25-21   32-11-44   15-53-45-25-54-25-34   52-44-45-44

32-11-44   42-54-31-32-11   21-41-14.

WHAT God SAYS TO THE SNOW

God **thunders** marvelously with His **voice**. He does **great things**, which we cannot **comprehend**. For He **says** to the **snow**, 'Be on the **earth**,' likewise to the **small rain** and to the **great** rain of His **strength**.

JOB 37:5–6 SKJV

SPOTTY HEADLINE

A●OSTL● WALKS ON WATE● WI●H J●SUS

Hint: He also later denied knowing Jesus.

——— —— —— —— ———

```
T  L  L  A  M  S  T  X  J  D
L  T  L  G  W  O  N  S  J  N
S  T  R  E  N  G  T  H  S  E
G  V  O  I  C  E  Q  R  B  H
T  R  A  H  G  R  E  A  T  E
B  R  E  C  T  D  W  N  H  R
K  D  F  A  N  R  S  K  I  P
N  O  C  U  T  A  A  M  N  M
J  G  H  N  Y  L  W  E  G  O
Y  T  H  S  Q  R  M  V  S  C
```

DAVid ANd GoliATH

1 SAMUEL 17:50 NLV

With God's help, David stared down a giant.
Crack the code to find out who won!

Goliath was a warrior of the _____
(1 Samuel 17:4).   12-22-25-38-32-19-15-24-36-5-16

Another word for slaves
(1 Samuel 17:9)   21-14-8-13-3-35-28-29

David cared for his father's _____
(1 Samuel 17:20)   37-20-18-33-11

David's brothers _____ Saul
(1 Samuel 17:13)   37-4-38-38-27-34-5-2

Saul tried giving some _____ to David
(1 Samuel 17:38 SKJV)   3-1-26-27-6

Goliath served many _____ (1 Samuel 17:43)   7-31-2-9

Goliath's _____ was used to finish
him off (1 Samuel 17:51)   30-34-4-17-10

16-4   10-3-13-25-2   34-31-35   15-22-14   37-32-7-22-28

3-7-3-24-35-9-28   28-22-5   12-22-24-20-25-21-28-32-35-14

34-25-15-22   3   9-20-25-35-7   3-35-2   3   9-15-27-36-14.

CLUES:

The ark builder (Genesis 7:9): N ____ ____ ____

Worship song (Matthew 26:30): ____ ____ ____ ____

One of four directions

(Luke 13:29): N ____ ____ ____ ____

Gideon
(Judges 6-8)

Across

4. The false god whose altar Gideon pulled down (6:25)

6. The false god whose tree Gideon cut down (6:25)

9. Number of sons Gideon had (8:30)

Down

1. Pets today, but not in Bible times (7:5)

2. What farmers grow (6:11 KJV)

3. What Gideon used to prove God was talking to him (6:37 KJV)

4. The kind of bread a Midianite dreamed of (7:13)

5. An expression of surprise

7. Used to hold water (7:20 NLV)

8. He was killed in a winepress (7:25 KJV)

SPOTTY HEADLINE

L●ONS LE●VE GO●'S
PROPH●T A●O●E

Hint: He was down in the den.

___ ___ ___ ___ ___ ___

CHOOSE YOUR FRIENDS CAREFULLY

Confidence in an **unfaithful** man in time of **trouble** is like a **broken tooth** and a **foot** out of **joint**. Like he who takes away a **garment** in **cold weather**, and like **vinegar** on soda, so is he who **sings** songs to a **heavy heart**.
PROVERBS 25:19–20 SKJV

SPOTTY HEADLINE

●IRACLE BU●H GET● PR●PHET'S ATT●NTION

Hint: He led the Israelites out of slavery in Egypt.

____ ____ ____ ____ ____

```
L E T G N T R S H J
U C R O F K G P O R
F N A D O N J I W F
H E G D I T N P E O
T D E S L T H L A O
I I N H C O B X T T
A F I E N U C L H M
F N V A O Y V A E H
N O B R O K E N R P
U C T T N E M R A G
```

JESUS' BUSY DAY

MATTHEW 14:33 NLV

Jesus and His disciples had an exciting day
full of unforgettable miracles. Crack the code
to see how the disciples responded!

The disciples told Jesus to send the crowd _____
(Matthew 14:15)   19-24-9-20

Jesus fed five _____ men
(Matthew 14:21)   23-1-30-3-38-33-18-29

_____ walked to Jesus on the water
(Matthew 14:29)   5-17-4-31-37

Peter was afraid when he saw the
_____ wind (Matthew 14:30 NLV)   22-6-11-35-36-10

_____ prevented Peter from sinking
(Matthew 14:31)   14-15-13-7-26

"O you of little _____" (Matthew 14:31 SKJV)
                                              34-2-28-37-12

Gets in the way of faith (Matthew 14:31)   8-16-25-32-21

4-1-35-13-17   28-18   6-12-31   32-30-19-21

24-16-11-26-1-28-5-15-29   14-31-38-3-13.   37-1-17-20

26-19-28-8, "34-16-11   22-25-11-15,   20-30-7   33-11-31

37-12-31   38-16-18   35-34   10-30-29!"

	1	2	3	4	5
1	N	A	P	O	Z
2	L	M	H	W	T
3	Y	U	I	E	J
4	V	C	B	K	Q
5	S	D	F	R	G

ROMANS 10:10 SKJV

53-14-54   24-33-25-23   25-23-34   23-34-12-54-25

22-12-11   43-34-21-33-34-41-34-51   25-14

54-33-55-23-25-34-14-32-51-11-34-51-51, 12-11-52   24-33-25-23

25-23-34   22-14-32-25-23   42-14-11-53-34-51-51-33-14-11   33-51

22-12-52-34   25-14   51-12-21-41-12-25-33-14-11.

PAUL IN EPHESUS (ACTS 19)

Across

1. Joined Timothy in helping Paul (verse 22)

4. A silversmith (verse 24)

7. Number of years Paul stayed in Ephesus (verse 10)

8. The man whose school Paul used (verse 9)

Down

2. Bad stuff that happens (verse 40 NLV)

3. Jumped on the sons of Sceva (verse 16 NLV)

4. False god worshipped by Ephesians (verse 28)

5. Where shows are performed (verse 29 SKJV)

6. Things you read (verse 19)

SCRAMBLED PLACE

RICH JOE

Hint: Both Joshua and Zacchaeus were there at some time.

___ ___ ___ ___ ___ ___ ___

God, The Weather Maker

He gives **snow** like **wool**. He **spreads** ice like **ashes**. He throws down **His ice** as **hail** stones. Who can **stand** before His **cold**? He sends out **His Word** and **melts** them. He makes His **wind blow** and the **waters flow**.

PSALM 147:16–18 NLV

SPOTTY HEADLINE

FIRST WIF● IS MOTH●R OF ALL LI●ING

Hint: She was made from her husband's rib.

___ ___ ___

```
D  W  Y  B  C  H  B  L  O  W
N  L  Z  V  F  I  J  D  V  M
A  L  O  L  F  S  N  D  T  E
W  S  O  C  H  I  T  R  L  L
A  W  H  A  W  C  T  O  W  T
T  Z  I  E  M  E  O  W  O  S
E  L  T  T  S  W  K  S  N  K
R  P  Z  M  T  J  L  I  S  P
S  P  R  E  A  D  S  H  G  B
R  M  R  K  D  N  A  T  S  L
```

CLUES:

First "little brother" (Genesis 4:1–2): A ___ ___ ___

Another word for "work"

(Matthew 11:28): ___ ___ ___ ___ ___

To gather crops (Luke 12:24): R ___ ___ ___ ___

CROSSING THE RED SEA

EXODUS 14:30 SKJV

The Israelites had left Egypt, but the
Egyptians weren't quite finished with them yet.
Crack the code to see how the story ends!

_____ tried to get the Israelites
back (Exodus 14:5)   29-30-20-3-10-28-17

Israel saw the _____ coming
(Exodus 14:10)   12-25-26-31-22-1-23-16-8

The cloud _____ light to Israel (Exodus 14:20)   9-4-7-11

The Egyptians _____ Israel
(Exodus 14:23 NLV)   15-13-21-6-14-27-5-18

Moses stretched _____ his hand
(Exodus 14:27 SKJV)   19-24-2

2-17-24-8   22-30-11   21-19-3-18   8-20-7-12-18   1-8-3-23-5-6

2-30-4-22   18-4-26   13-24-22   14-15   2-17-11   30-4-16-18   28-15

22-30-5   11-9-26-29-2-1-20-16-8,   23-16-18   1-8-3-20-12-21

8-10-27   22-17-12   5-25-26-31-2-1-10-16-8   18-12-20-18   19-16

22-17-5   8-11-4-8-30-14-3-11.

THe Life of PeTeR

Across

3. A living alarm clock (Luke 22:60)

4. The "body of Christ" (Matthew 16:18)

7. Professional warriors (Acts 12:6)

8. What Peter once did for a living (John 21:3)

Down

1. What Peter found empty (Luke 24:12 NLV)

2. Languages, both earthly and heavenly (Acts 2:4 KJV)

5. Who Peter said Jesus was (Luke 9:20)

6. Another name for Peter (Luke 5:8)

SPOTTY HEADLINE

●OTHER OF JESUS IS
●OUNG ●ND UNMA●RIED

*Hint: Sometimes we sing about her
during the Christmas season.*

___ ___ ___ ___

SHEPHERD PSALM

The **Lord** is my **Shepherd**. I will have everything I **need**. He lets me **rest** in **fields** of **green grass**. He leads me beside the **quiet waters**. He makes me **strong** again. He <u>leads me</u> in the way of **living** right with Himself which brings **honor** to <u>**His name**</u>.

PSALM 23:1–3 NLV

SCRAMBLED PLACE

A SUD SCAM

Hint: Saul was saved on the road to this city.

___ ___ ___ ___ ___ ___ ___ ___

H L E A D S M E N G
N L M S S A R G N G
R Y A S M L F O R D
C E N R R T R E R R
K F S E K T E E F O
R I I T S N H I M L
O E H A G P L N U J
N L R W E D W V L Q
O D G H L I V I N G
H S S R N E E D L C

ELIJAH AND THE PROPHETS OF BAAL

1 KINGS 18:38 SKJV

The prophet Elijah hosted an earth-shattering competition to see whose god was the true God. Crack the code to find out how it ended!

King _____ hated Elijah (1 Kings 18:17)
15-5-18-2

The prophets gathered on Mount _____
(1 Kings 18:20)
17-32-30-6-11-24

The people's reply to Elijah: It is well _____
(1 Kings 18:24 SKJV)
27-1-9-37-7-14

Sharp objects used in war
(1 Kings 18:28 NLV)
8-40-23-41-19-13

Elijah used twelve _____ to build an altar
(1 Kings 18:31)
35-31-4-20-36-29

Elijah cut a _____ in pieces (1 Kings 18:33)
25-39-26-33

Elijah had watered poured on
the _____ (1 Kings 18:33 SKJV)
21-22-16-12-38-10-3-28-34

31-5-11-20 31-5-34 10-38-41-7 9-10 31-5-11 26-4-30-19

10-36-24-33 22-14-19 16-23-20-8-39-6-11-19 31-5-36

25-39-30-20-31 35-22-17-30-3-10-38-17-36 32-20-19 31-5-7

40-23-4-19 18-14-19 31-5-34 8-31-9-20-7-8 32-14-19

31-5-36 19-39-21-31, 15-20-19 24-38-17-37-36-19 39-1

31-5-11 40-15-31-36-12 31-5-18-31 40-32-13 3-14 31-5-34

31-12-7-20-17-5.

	1	2	3	4	5
1	R	G	F	B	E
2	W	C	U	L	S
3	T	I	X	A	N
4	K	O	M	J	D
5	Z	H	Y	P	V

GALATIANS 4:31 SKJV

25-42   31-52-15-35,   14-11-42-31-52-15-11-25,   21-15   34-11-15

22-52-32-24-45-11-15-35   35-42-31   42-13   31-52-15

14-42-35-45-21-42-43-34-35   14-23-31   42-13   31-52-15

13-11-15-15.

35

BALAAM'S BiG SURPRiSe

NUMBERS 23:5 SKJV

Balaam was sent to curse Israel. . .but God got his
attention through an angel and a talking donkey!
Crack the code to see what happened next!

King _____ sent Balaam to curse Israel
(Numbers 22:10)   27-15-22-17-21

To slow down or stop
(Numbers 22:16 SKJV)   18-30-35-8-31-19

Balaam saddled his _____ and left
(Numbers 22:21)   12-32-28-24-33-29

The donkey _____ herself against the wall
(Numbers 22:25 SKJV)   34-4-26-3-6-13

Balaam wished for a _____ to kill his donkey
(Numbers 22:29)   14-7-11-5-10

Balak offered to _____ Balaam
(Numbers 22:37 SKJV)   20-16-2-1-25-9-23

15-28-10   9-18-33   22-32-5-12   20-3-13   17   7-11-16-8   30-28

27-17-22-15-15-1-'6   1-2-3-34-4   17-28-8   14-15-30-10,

"5-31-13-3-26-28   9-25   27-17-22-15-21,   17-28-12   34-4-3-14

29-11-3   6-18-15-22-22   14-20-33-17-24."

CLUES:

Important Bible writer (Philemon 19): P ___ ___ ___

What the devil is (John 8:44): ___ ___ ___ ___

To give back (Romans 12:19): R ___ ___ ___ ___

God Keeps Snow in a Store-House?

"Have you **gone** into the **store**-houses of the **snow**? Have you seen the store-**houses** of the **hail**, which I have **kept** for the **time** of **trouble**, for the day of **war** and **battle**? What is the way to the **place** where the **light** is **divided**, or the <u>east wind</u> spread over the **earth**?"

JOB 38:22–24 NLV

SPOTTY HEADLINE

M●N IN GAR●EN N●MES THE ANI●ALS

Hint: The first man! (C'mon, do you really need a hint for this one?)

____ ____ ____ ____

```
J  Q  W  L  I  G  H  T  E  V
S  N  O  W  E  N  B  C  C  J
X  H  T  R  A  E  A  L  E  T
R  N  O  R  K  L  D  T  L  R
H  T  R  E  P  E  M  I  T  O
S  O  P  A  D  N  D  H  T  U
Q  T  U  I  W  O  T  A  A  B
Q  Y  V  S  N  G  Y  I  B  L
G  I  V  D  E  B  P  L  T  E
D  N  I  W  T  S  A  E  M  R
```

NOAH AND THE ARK (GENESIS 6-9)

Across

1. Number of days it rained (7:12)

4. Type of leaf the dove brought back (8:11)

5. Creator of everything (6:9)

7. Super high hills (7:19 NLV)

9. They walked the earth before the Flood (6:4 SKJV)

Down

1. What you get when it rains too much (6:17)

2. Colors in the sky after it rains (9:13 NLV)

3. What the earth was full of before the Flood (6:11 SKJV)

6. Where the ark landed (8:4)

8. One of Noah's sons (9:18)

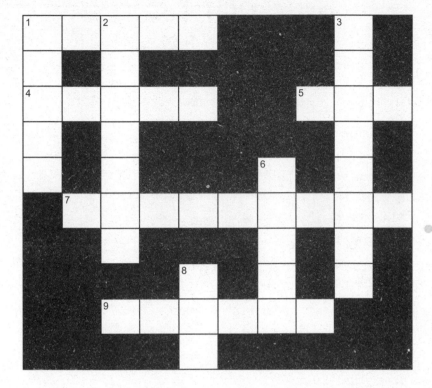

SPOTTY HEADLINE

FAIT●F●L LE●DER
DEFEAT● ●ERICH●

Hint: He was Moses' assistant.

___ ___ ___ ___ ___ ___

RUTH

RUTH 4:17 SKJV

Ruth's story is far more than just a love story—
it's an important part of Israel's history.
Crack the code to find out how!

Naomi and Ruth went to _____
(Ruth 1:19)   42-31-17-29-1-3-9-25-28

A woman who is from Moab
(Ruth 1:22 KJV)   8-41-32-14-33-10-4-40-23

"_____ have I found favor in your eyes?"
(Ruth 2:10 NLV)   7-37-22

Boaz let some grain _____ for Ruth
(Ruth 2:16 KJV)   19-5-16-43

Ruth _____ in the field (Ruth 2:17 KJV)   35-20-30-2-24-12-13

Ruth took the _____ off Boaz's feet
(Ruth 3:7 NLV)   11-39-6-18-34-27

David's dad (Ruth 4:22)   15-38-36-21-26

32-24-13 17-9-4 7-41-28-31-24, 37-18-34

24-30-33-35-29-42-39-34-36, 35-32-6-26 33-10 5

24-32-8-18, 27-2-22-33-24-35, "17-37-4-34-38 33-21

32 27-39-24 14-41-34-24 10-39 24-32-41-28-33,"

5-24-13 17-9-4-22 11-32-1-16-30-13 9-33-40 24-2-8-18

39-42-30-13. 29-4 33-23 17-37-3 19-32-17-37-30-34

41-19 15-31-40-27-4, 10-37-30 19-5-10-9-18-34 39-19

13-32-6-33-13.

DECODER

	1	2	3	4	5
1	I	V	S	O	E
2	D	K	H	G	B
3	U	R	W	F	T
4	P	L	X	A	Y
5	J	Z	C	N	M

JOHN 3:16 SKJV

34-14-32 24-14-21 13-14 42-14-12-15-21 35-23-15

33-14-32-42-21 35-23-44-35 23-15 24-44-12-15 23-11-13

14-54-42-45 25-15-24-14-35-35-15-54 13-14-54, 35-23-44-35

33-23-14-15-12-15-32 25-15-42-11-15-12-15-13 11-54 23-11-55

13-23-14-31-42-21 54-14-35 41-15-32-11-13-23 25-31-35

23-44-12-15 15-12-15-32-42-44-13-35-11-54-24

42-11-34-15.

A PRAYER FROM A FISH'S BELLY

When my **soul fainted** within me, I **remembered** the LORD,
and my **prayer** came in to You, into Your **holy temple**.
Those who observe **lying** vanities forsake their own **mercy**.
But I will **sacrifice** to You with the **voice** of thanksgiving.
I will pay what I have **vowed**. **Salvation** is of the LORD.
JONAH 2:7–9 SKJV

SPOTTY HEADLINE

●ELFISH ●NGEL
W●STES PERFEC●IO●

Hint: Another name for the devil.

___ ___ ___ ___

```
T  S  A  L  V  A  T  I  O  N
Y  E  C  I  F  I  R  C  A  S
R  E  M  E  M  B  E  R  E  D
L  G  M  V  O  W  E  D  E  H
L  K  N  L  Y  C  V  T  O  P
U  O  X  I  I  D  N  L  Y  R
O  Y  R  O  Y  I  Y  R  C  A
S  K  V  D  A  L  C  V  R  Y
V  Y  K  F  K  Y  B  F  E  E
W  E  L  P  M  E  T  B  M  R
```

45

	1	2	3	4	5
1	B	N	Z	C	T
2	I	G	W	F	Y
3	U	D	H	X	V
4	L	O	P	Q	A
5	S	M	R	K	E

COLOSSIANS 3:15 SKJV

45-12-32   41-55-15   15-33-55   43-55-45-14-55   42-24

22-42-32   53-31-41-55   21-12   25-42-31-53   33-55-45-53-15-51,

15-42   23-33-21-14-33   25-42-31   45-41-51-42   45-53-55

14-45-41-41-55-32   21-12   42-12-55   11-42-32-25.

45-12-32   11-55   15-33-45-12-54-24-31-41.

CLUES:

What swallowed Jonah (Jonah 1:17): F ____ ____ ____

Divided by two (Luke 19:8): ____ ____ ____ ____

A hard challenge (1 Timothy 6:12): F ____ ____ ____ ____

SNOW IN SUMMERTIME?

Like **snow** in **summer** and like **rain** at **gathering** time, so **honor** is not right for a **fool**. Like a **sparrow** in its traveling, like a **swallow** in its **flying**, so bad **words** said against someone without **reason** do not come to **rest**. A **whip** is for the **horse**, leather ropes are for the **donkey**, and a **stick** is for the back of fools.

PROVERBS 26:1–3 NLV

SPOTTY HEADLINE

FIS●ERMA● F●LLOWS ●ESUS

Hint: There's a book of the Bible named for him.

___ ___ ___ ___

G	B	W	O	R	R	A	P	S	R
W	A	N	S	E	E	H	F	F	M
H	W	T	M	D	O	S	O	N	W
I	Y	M	H	R	R	O	T	O	H
P	U	E	S	E	L	O	L	S	O
S	Z	E	K	L	R	L	W	A	N
T	R	A	I	N	A	I	O	E	O
I	Y	Y	P	W	O	W	N	R	R
C	M	L	S	M	H	D	S	G	N
K	H	F	L	Y	I	N	G	H	H

49

PAUL'S TRIP TO ROME

ACTS 28:30 SKJV

For preaching Jesus, Paul was arrested and shipped off to Rome. . .and he had more than a few problems along the way. Crack the code to find out how the story ends!

Paul's ship sailed past _____ because
the winds were bad (Acts 27:4)　　　　29-2-24-32-17-30

Leader of a hundred soldiers
(Acts 27:6 KJV)　　　　1-7-16-33-21-11-23-6-8

Fair _____ was near the city
of Lasea (Acts 27:8)　　　　22-34-3-27-19-5

The soldiers didn't want the prisoners
to _____ away (Acts 27:42)　　　　9-20-18-13

Everyone washed up on the island
of _____ (Acts 28:1)　　　　10-25-31-26-4

A snake bit Paul's _____ (Acts 28:3)　　　　12-28-14-15

34-16-15　24-25-21-31　15-20-7-31-31-27-15　26-20-6

20-22-6-31-7　2-27-4-11-30　18-8　22-23-5　6-20-14

22-18-32-27-15　22-6-21-9-7,　34-8-15　11-27-1-27-23-3-7-15

34-31-31　20-22-6　1-34-13-27　26-6　22-18-13.

	1	2	3	4	5
1	P	S	A	R	T
2	B	W	K	I	J
3	Y	V	H	C	X
4	O	G	Z	F	E
5	U	M	D	L	N

PROVERBS 1:7 SKJV

15-33-45 44-45-13-14 41-44 15-33-45 54-41-14-53

24-12 15-33-45 21-45-42-24-55-55-24-55-42 41-44

23-55-41-22-54-45-53-42-45, 21-51-15 44-41-41-54-12

53-45-12-11-24-12-45 22-24-12-53-41-52 13-55-53

24-55-12-15-14-51-34-15-24-41-55.

God's Word

Across

1. It's compared to this food (Matthew 4:4)

2. Spotless; innocent (Proverbs 31:5 SKJV)

4. Another word for the Bible (2 Timothy 3:15 SKJV)

7. Amount of God's words that fail (Ezekiel 12:28)

8. This person should live by God's Word (Psalm 119:9)

Down

1. The Word was here (John 1:1)

2. What God's Word will never do (Matthew 5:18)

3. How the Word affects hearts (Hebrews 4:12 SKJV)

5. God's Word is like this in a person's life (1 Peter 1:23)

6. Who gives all the Holy Writings (2 Timothy 3:16)

SCRAMBLED PLACE

HEN VINE

Hint: It's where Jonah was trying not to go!

___ ___ ___ ___ ___ ___ ___

A JOB FOR JEREMIAH

Now the **Word** of the **Lord** came to me saying, "Before I **started** to put you **together** in your **mother**, I knew you. Before you were **born**, I set you apart as **holy**. I **chose** you to **speak** to the nations for Me." Then I said, "O, Lord God! I do not know how to speak. I am <u>only a boy</u>." But the Lord said to me, "Do not say, 'I am only a boy.' You **must** go everywhere I **send** you. And you must say **whatever** I tell you."

JEREMIAH 1:4–7 NLV

SPOTTY HEADLINE

●ISCIPLE ●ORKS I● SH●DOW
OF MOR● FAMOUS B●OTHER

Hint: The more famous brother was Peter.

—— —— —— —— —— ——

```
J  N  T  M  E  L  M  B  R  B
W  K  N  O  M  S  Y  L  O  H
H  X  N  T  G  R  O  R  J  D
A  P  K  H  D  E  N  H  R  P
T  V  A  E  R  P  T  O  C  R
E  F  E  R  O  V  L  H  T  L
V  N  P  T  W  J  S  G  E  Y
E  Z  S  T  A  R  T  E  D  R
R  U  M  T  Y  K  H  C  N  M
M  O  N  L  Y  A  B  O  Y  D
```

JoSHUA ANd THe WALLS oF JeRicHo

JOSHUA 6:27 SKJV

God gave Joshua some pretty odd instructions
for how to conquer Jericho. Crack the code
to see what happened to Joshua next!

God had given _____ into Joshua's hand
(Joshua 6:2)   21-25-3-4-8-19-24

The priests were to blow the _____
(Joshua 6:4 KJV)   1-14-11-12-6-20-23-13

Israel rose on the _____ of the
seventh day (Joshua 6:15 KJV)   15-22-18-16-29-9-10

The walls fell down _____ (Joshua 6:20 KJV)   7-5-26-2

Rahab hid the men who were sent to _____
on Jericho (Joshua 6:25)   28-17-27

13-24   1-19-20   5-24-14-15   18-22-28   18-4-23-19

21-24-13-19-11-26,   22-16-15   19-29-13   7-22-12-25   18-26-28

3-25-17-24-14-2-20-15   1-19-14-24-11-10-19-24-11-2   26-5-5

23-19-25   8-24-11-16-23-3-27.

CLUES:

The first woman (Genesis 3:20): E ____ ____

A word meaning "all" (Matthew 4:4):

____ ____ ____ ____ ____

Not old (Titus 2:4, 6): Y ____ ____ ____ ____

RAIN, SNOW, GOD'S WORD

"The **rain** and **snow** come down from **heaven** and do not return there without **giving water** to the **earth**. This makes **plants grow** on the earth, and gives **seeds** to the planter and **bread** to the **eater**. So <u>My Word</u> which goes from My **mouth** will not return to Me **empty**. It will do what I want it to do, and will carry out My **plan** well."

ISAIAH 55:10–11 NLV

SPOTTY HEADLINE

⬤ISCIPLE T⬤RNS
⬤GAIN⬤T ⬤ESUS!

Hint: He betrayed Jesus with a kiss.

___ ___ ___ ___ ___

```
H  R  G  C  H  E  A  V  E  N
T  E  W  I  Y  T  K  B  N  P
U  A  A  X  V  T  V  V  I  L
O  T  T  B  W  I  P  N  A  A
M  E  E  T  Z  W  N  M  R  N
H  R  R  D  O  E  O  G  E  S
L  S  T  N  A  L  P  R  M  D
Y  F  S  R  W  J  V  P  G  E
W  M  T  N  D  A  E  R  B  E
L  H  D  R  O  W  Y  M  L  S
```

DECODER

	1	2	3	4	5
1	N	R	G	M	T
2	C	W	O	J	U
3	V	I	Y	E	Z
4	F	H	L	S	X
5	B	K	P	D	A

EXODUS 20:4 NLV

"54-23 11-23-15 14-55-52-34 41-23-12

33-23-25-12-44-34-43-31-34-44 55 13-23-54 15-23

43-23-23-52 43-32-52-34 55-11-33-15-42-32-11-13

15-42-55-15 32-44 32-11 42-34-55-31-34-11 55-51-23-31-34

23-12 23-11 15-42-34 34-55-12-15-42 51-34-43-23-22 23-12

32-11 15-42-34 22-55-15-34-12-44 25-11-54-34-12 15-42-34

34-55-12-15-42."

ESTHER

ESTHER 7:10 SKJV

Evil Haman plotted to kill all the Jews. . .
but his plan backfired spectacularly!
Crack the code to see how his story ended.

Esther's cousin who adopted her
(Esther 2:7)   12-5-16-8-31-23-9-21

King Ahasuerus chose _____ to be
queen (Esther 2:17)   10-26-4-27-11-22

The king held out his _____ to Esther
(Esther 5:2 SKJV)   1-29-33-6-34-17-14

"The adversary and enemy is this _____
Haman" (Esther 7:6 KJV)   35-20-28-37-15-32

Esther couldn't bear seeing her _____
destroyed (Esther 8:6 SKJV)   18-25-2-19-3-36

Laws were sealed with the king's
_____ (Esther 8:8)   24-13-30-7

1-5   34-27-10-36   27-9-30-7-31-32   27-25-12-9-30   5-30

34-27-15   7-9-3-3-5-35-26   4-27-25-34   27-31   27-25-32

6-22-31-6-25-14-10-32   18-5-14   12-5-22-32-11-29-25-20.

34-27-31-30   4-27-33   37-19-30-7-'1   25-30-7-10-22   35-9-26

6-25-29-20-18-21-11-32.

THe CReATION (GeNeSiS 1)

Across

3. Live in the sea (verse 28)

4. What humans have over nature (verse 26 SKJV)

6. Created on the first day (verse 3)

8. What farmers raise (verse 24)

Down

1. Things that fly (verse 20 NLV)

2. It divided the waters (verse 6 SKJV)

3. Grows on trees (verse 11)

5. What God created everything from (verse 1 NLV)

7. Opposite of night (verse 16)

SPOTTY HEADLINE

SHEPHER● BOY ●EFE●TS E●IL G●ANT

Hint: The boy later became king.

___ ___ ___ ___ ___

TWELVE APOSTLES

Now the names of the **twelve apostles** are these: the first, **Simon**, who is called **Peter**, and **Andrew** his brother; **James** the son of Zebedee, and **John** his brother; **Philip**, and Bartholomew; **Thomas**, and **Matthew** the **tax** collector; James the son of Alphaeus, and **Lebbaeus**, whose surname was Thaddaeus; Simon the Canaanite and **Judas** Iscariot, who also **betrayed** Him.

MATTHEW 10:2–4 SKJV

SPOTTY HEADLINE

TAL●, H●NDSOME G●Y NAMED KING OF I●RAEL

Hint: There's a guy by the same name in the New Testament too.

___ ___ ___ ___

```
T  L  E  B  B  A  E  U  S  S
G  F  N  H  O  J  Q  F  E  M
S  I  M  O  N  X  C  L  F  W
B  D  E  Y  A  R  T  E  B  E
S  E  P  T  L  S  H  R  A  H
A  V  Z  I  O  P  J  K  N  T
M  L  M  P  L  A  E  Q  D  T
O  E  A  Z  M  I  K  T  R  A
H  W  J  E  R  J  H  H  E  M
T  T  S  A  D  U  J  P  W  R
```

DECODER

	1	2	3	4	5
1	L	E	G	U	N
2	W	D	F	H	O
3	Q	A	J	P	T
4	K	R	S	C	M
5	I	Y	B	V	X

Ecclesiastes 3:1 skjv

35-24-12-42-12   51-43   32   43-12-32-43-25-15   23-25-42

12-54-12-42-52-35-24-51-15-13   32-15-22   32   35-51-45-12

23-25-42   12-54-12-42-52   34-14-42-34-25-43-12

14-15-22-12-42   24-12-32-54-12-15.

CLUES:

Another name for Jerusalem (Isaiah 30:19): Z ___ ___ ___

Loud sounds (2 Peter 3:10): ___ ___ ___ ___ ___

Wanting what others have (James 4:5): E ___ ___ ___

AFTER WINTER, SPRING

My **beloved** spoke and said to me, "<u>Rise up</u>, my love, my **beautiful** one, and <u>come away</u>. For, behold, the **winter** is **past**. The **rain** is over and gone. The **flowers** appear on the **earth**. The **time** of the **singing** of **birds** has come, and the **voice** of the turtledove is **heard** in our land."

SONG OF SOLOMON 2:10–12 SKJV

SCRAMBLED PLACE

NEED OF DANGER

Hint: Think Adam and Eve

___ ___ ___ ___ ___ ___ ___ ___

___ ___ ___ ___

```
B  E  A  U  T  I  F  U  L  T
Z  Y  E  H  T  R  A  E  P  R
J  A  T  M  A  Z  S  V  P  D
S  W  P  I  I  D  D  U  G  W
R  A  N  A  R  T  E  D  N  I
E  E  B  I  S  S  V  R  I  N
W  M  B  L  I  T  O  A  G  T
O  O  K  R  L  L  L  E  N  E
L  C  D  C  Q  M  E  H  I  R
F  V  O  I  C  E  B  L  S  N
```

SAMSON

JUDGES 16:29 SKJV

Samson was a mighty man who, with God's help, managed to bring down a bunch of Israel's enemies—even with his last breath. Crack the code to find out how Samson won his last victory.

Samson saw a _____ in Timnah
(Judges 14:1)　　　　　　　　　4-36-16-29-26

Looked for; searched (Judges 14:4 KJV)　　34-41-19-5-35-3

Samson saw a lion's _____ beside the
road (Judges 14:8 SKJV)　　　　8-42-28-32-39-33-13

A tricky question (Judges 14:12 KJV)　　43-23-38-25-31-9

The _____ killed Samson's wife
(Judges 15:6)　　　22-24-17-40-10-1-6-7-21-44-20

Samson would be _____ if his hair were cut
(Judges 16:17)　　　　　　　　　30-11-14-37

The Philistines gathered to _____ a sacrifice
(Judges 16:23 KJV)　　　　　　　12-27-18-15-2

42-26-38　34-29-16-33-41-21　3-36-12-37　24-36-31-25　41-18

3-24-44　6-4-12　16-17-25-38-40-11　22-10-40-31-39-43-1

12-26　30-35-23-8-24　3-24-9　35-36-19-20-15　13-6-41-36-38,

39-26-25　12-26　30-35-17-32-35　7-3　30-29-13　24-44-31-38

19-22,　12-18　6-35-9　36-21-15　4-17-3-24　24-7-1　2-23-5-24-3

35-39-21-25　29-26-38　12-18　6-24-11　12-3-35-15-28

30-17-3-24　35-7-20　40-9-18-6.

	1	2	3	4	5
1	K	J	T	D	Y
2	H	L	V	P	C
3	I	O	R	E	Z
4	U	F	N	M	G
5	X	S	W	B	A

ACTS 2:38 NLV

24-34-13-34-33 52-55-31-14 13-32 13-21-34-44,

"54-34 52-32-33-33-15 42-32-33 15-32-41-33

52-31-43-52 55-43-14 13-41-33-43 42-33-32-44

13-21-34-44 55-43-14 54-34 54-55-24-13-31-35-34-14

31-43 13-21-34 43-55-44-34 32-42 12-34-52-41-52

25-21-33-31-52-13, 55-43-14 15-32-41-33 52-31-43-52

53-31-22-22 54-34 42-32-33-45-31-23-34-43. 15-32-41

53-31-22-22 33-34-25-34-31-23-34 13-21-34 45-31-42-13

32-42 13-21-34 21-32-22-15 52-24-31-33-31-13."

OLD TESTAMENT MIRACLES

Answer

2. The second-to-last plague on Egypt (Exodus 10:22)

4. Where Moses struck a rock to get water (Exodus 17:6)

6. Elijah built one when defeating Baal's prophets (1 Kings 18:32)

8. What Shadrach and his friends survived (Daniel 3:19 SKJV)

9. It stood still for Joshua (Joshua 10:12)

Down

1. Naaman did this to be rid of his skin disease (2 Kings 5:10)

3. This river parted for Joshua (Joshua 3:15)

5. He heard his donkey speak (Numbers 22:28)

7. Elisha made this metal float (2 Kings 6:6)

SPOTTY HEADLINE

ANGRY ●IANT L●SES ●IS
HE●D ●N BA●T●E

Hint: Little David's big opponent.

___ ___ ___ ___ ___ ___ ___

WALKING ON WATER!

Peter said to **Jesus**, "If it is You, **Lord**, tell me to **come** to You on the **water**." Jesus said, "Come!" Peter got out of the **boat** and **walked** on the water to Jesus. But when he saw the **strong wind**, he was **afraid**. He began to go down in the water. He <u>**cried out**</u>, "Lord, <u>**save me**</u>!" At once Jesus put out His **hand** and took hold of him. Jesus said to Peter, "You have so little **faith**! Why did you **doubt**?"
MATTHEW 14:28–31 NLV

SPOTTY HEADLINE

M●SES' B●OTHER N●MED PRIEST I● ISR●EL

Hint: He made a big mistake making the golden calf.

___ ___ ___ ___ ___

```
T U O D E I R C D F
H G Q F N D H I V J
F N X P O I A J S W
A O R U C R W U R A
I R B W F O S Q E T
T T G A M E M Q T E
H S M K J B H E E R
L O R D O X Z A P M
T B S A V E M E N B
L G T D E K L A W D
```

JeSUS TURNS WATER INTO WINE

JOHN 2:11 SKJV

Jesus performed an unforgettable miracle at a wedding one day. Crack the code to see why this miracle was so special—and what His disciples did in response!

Cana was in _____ (John 2:1)   9-14-21-31-13-7-27

Jesus' _____ went with Him to the
wedding (John 2:2 KJV)   35-6-45-2-15-16-46-20-37

Jesus' _____ was at the wedding
(John 2:3)   1-47-11-10-39-28

Jesus' mother told the _____ to obey
Him (John 2:5 KJV)   29-32-17-25-4-42-23-41

There were six _____ at the wedding
(John 2:6 NLV)   33-30-40-8

Cleansing; making clean
(John 2:6 KJV)   22-5-19-26-18-36-12-38-3

They filled the pots to the _____
John 2:7 (KJV)   43-44-24-34

23-10-31-45   43-20-9-12-42-38-6-42-9   47-18

34-15-40-14-2-21-32-37   33-7-29-5-8   35-15-35   26-42

2-14-42-30   47-18   3-4-21-6-13-32-39   30-38-35

17-20-25-7-4-13-20-35   10-12-8   9-21-47-28-36.   14-42-35

10-24-45   35-12-29-2-31-22-13-32-8   43-39-21-6-32-25-20-35

24-38   10-31-1.

CLUES:

Opposite of rich (Mark 12:43): P ___ ___ ___

A plant's base (Matthew 13:6): ___ ___ ___ ___

Jesus will return like one

   (Revelation 16:15): T ___ ___ ___ ___

A WINTER HOLIDAY

And it was the **Feast** of the Dedication in **Jerusalem**, and it was **winter**. And **Jesus walked** in the **temple** in Solomon's **porch**. Then the **Jews** came around Him and **said** to Him, "How long do You make us to **doubt**? If You are the **Christ**, tell us **plainly**." Jesus answered them, "I told you, and you do not **believe**."

JOHN 10:22–25 SKJV

SPOTTY HEADLINE

OLD WOM●N LAUG●● AT IDEA OF BI●THING B●BY

Hint: She was Abraham's wife.

___ ___ ___ ___ ___

H	C	R	O	P	L	D	T	R	W
Y	R	J	C	H	R	I	S	T	M
L	E	V	E	I	L	E	B	E	D
N	D	K	P	S	T	R	L	W	W
I	I	H	R	E	U	A	Z	A	T
A	A	F	M	S	S	S	T	L	S
L	S	P	T	U	W	B	R	K	A
P	L	L	R	K	U	E	F	E	E
E	N	E	P	O	W	K	J	D	F
K	J	V	D	W	I	N	T	E	R

	1	2	3	4	5
1	O	Z	M	Y	H
2	J	G	W	F	R
3	N	L	U	C	D
4	X	K	T	A	S
5	E	V	I	P	B

REVELATION 21:2 SKJV

44-31-35 53, 21-11-15-31, 45-44-23 43-15-51 15-11-32-14

34-53-43-14, 31-51-23 21-51-25-33-45-44-32-51-13,

34-11-13-53-31-22 35-11-23-31 11-33-43 11-24

15-51-44-52-51-31 24-25-11-13 22-11-35,

54-25-51-54-44-25-51-35 44-45 44 55-25-53-35-51

44-35-11-25-31-51-35 24-11-25 15-51-25

15-33-45-55-44-31-35.

	1	2	3	4	5
1	Z	Y	J	E	F
2	B	O	H	N	U
3	P	K	S	D	R
4	V	C	I	X	L
5	G	M	A	W	T

GENESIS 1:1 SKJV

43-24 55-23-14 21-14-51-43-24-24-43-24-51 51-22-34

42-35-14-53-55-14-34 55-23-14 23-14-53-41-14-24

53-24-34 55-23-14 14-53-35-55-23.

THE FAITH "HALL OF FAME" (HEBREWS 11)

Across

3. He believed God could raise the dead (verse 19)

5. Cain's brother (verse 4)

7. He never died (verse 5)

8. This happened before many heroes could see God's promises fulfilled (verse 13)

9. A boy almost sacrificed (verse 17)

Down

1. With God's help, Joshua brought its walls down (verse 30)

2. He's named with Gideon and Samson (verse 32)

4. The heroes would be made this (verse 40)

6. What many heroes lived in (verse 9)

M●RA●LE BABY'● PARENTS
●RE NINETY AND ● HUNDRED!

Hint: Later he was almost sacrificed on an altar.

___ ___ ___ ___ ___

ONE BiG MiSTAKe

A man by the name of **Ananias** and his wife, Sapphira, sold some **land**. He **kept back** part of the **money** for himself. His **wife** knew it also. The other **part** he took to the missionaries. **Peter** said to Ananias, "Why did you let **Satan** fill your heart? He made you <u>lie to</u> the **Holy Spirit**. You kept back part of the money you got from your land. Was not the land yours before you sold it? After it was **sold**, you could have done what you wanted to do with the money. Why did you allow your **heart** to do this? You have lied to **God**, not to men." When Ananias heard these words, he fell down **dead**.

ACTS 5:1–5 NLV

SCRAMBLED PERSON

BOAT MIGHT SOUND

Hint: A disciple with questions. . .

—— —— —— —— —— —— ——

—— —— —— —— —— ——

```
L  R  L  S  O  L  D  Q  C  Y
L  I  E  T  O  N  N  R  M  L
J  T  N  T  A  Z  A  M  D  O
X  K  R  L  E  Q  T  O  S  H
R  T  R  A  P  P  A  N  A  S
B  M  B  D  E  T  S  E  I  P
F  L  A  A  K  H  W  Y  N  I
K  E  P  T  C  I  H  D  A  R
D  X  K  D  F  K  O  V  N  I
T  Q  T  E  Z  G  B  P  A  T
```

THE RESURRECTION

JOHN 21:24 SKJV

Jesus' resurrection was the most important
event in history! Crack the code to find out
who's the one writing about it in this Gospel.

Mary _____ came to Jesus' tomb
(John 20:1)   11-20-8-24-4-17-23-10-26

Another word for tomb
(John 20:1 SKJV)   14-37-19-7-2-9-39-13-22

The two angels were dressed in _____
(John 20:12)   25-28-32-33-38

Another name for Thomas
(John 20:24 SKJV)   34-40-1-31-12-21-3

Jesus told Thomas to put his _____
into His hands (John 20:27)   30-36-16-35-5-15

Peter to Jesus: "You _____ that I love
You" (John 21:15)   27-18-6-29

33-39-36-14 40-3 33-28-26 34-32-14-9-40-19-17-22

29-39-6 33-23-3-33-36-30-32-5-14 6-30 33-28-5-3-38

33-28-40-16-8-14, 20-10-1 25-13-6-33-5 33-28-38-14-22

33-28-36-10-35-3, 20-16-34 25-26 27-10-6-25 33-28-4-33

39-36-14 33-5-14-33-40-12-6-16-31 40-3 33-15-21-22.

CLUES:

Mountain where Moses met with God (Exodus 19:20):

S ___ ___ ___ ___

God's name for Himself (Exodus 3:14): ___ ___ ___

Made with instruments (2 Chronicles 7:6):

M ___ ___ ___ ___

HABAKKUK'S PROMISE

"Although the **fig tree** shall not **blossom**, fruit shall not be on the **vines**, the labor of the **olive** shall fail, the **fields** shall yield no **food**, the **flock** shall be cut off from the **fold**, and there shall be no herd in the **stalls**, yet I will **rejoice** in the LORD. I will rejoice in the God of my **salvation**. The LORD God is my **strength**, and He will make my **feet** like deer's feet, and He will make me walk on my **high** places."

HABAKKUK 3:17–19 SKJV

SPOTTY HEADLINE

FATHER ●F TWELVE ●OYS ST●RTS MA●OR NEW ●OUNTRY

Hint: He stole his twin brother's blessing.

___ ___ ___ ___ ___

88

K	C	O	L	F	D	F	M	V	S
H	I	G	H	R	O	O	M	L	A
S	D	L	O	O	S	S	F	R	L
D	T	L	D	S	E	L	I	E	V
O	K	R	O	T	E	L	E	J	A
R	L	L	E	F	R	A	L	O	T
J	B	I	R	N	T	T	D	I	I
Z	C	M	V	T	G	S	S	C	O
F	E	E	T	E	I	T	X	E	N
V	I	N	E	S	F	M	H	M	R

	1	2	3	4	5
1	V	W	A	C	S
2	F	E	K	U	D
3	J	X	H	Z	B
4	T	Y	P	R	M
5	N	O	G	I	L

1 CORINTHIANS 13:1 NLV

54 45-13-42 35-22 13-35-55-22 41-52 15-43-22-13-23

41-33-22 55-13-51-53-24-13-53-22-15 52-21 45-22-51

13-51-25 22-11-22-51 52-21 13-51-53-22-55-15, 35-24-41

54-21 54 25-52 51-52-41 33-13-11-22 55-52-11-22, 54-41

12-54-55-55 15-52-24-51-25 55-54-23-22 51-52-54-15-42

35-44-13-15-15.

THE TEN PLAGUES ON EGYPT

EXODUS 12:31 NLV

Because Pharaoh wouldn't let God's people go,
God sent Egypt ten terrible plagues. Crack the code
to find out if Pharaoh ever changed his mind!

The _____ were able to copy the
first plague (Exodus 7:22 KJV)   26-36-20-1-16-11-37-13-14

Hopping animals (Exodus 8:2)   18-30-3-35-10

"Only you shall not go very far _____"
(Exodus 8:28 SKJV)   38-17-6-33

Hail didn't fall on the _____ of Israel
(Exodus 9:26 KJV)   34-19-9-8-7-39-29-32

The east wind _____ the locusts
(Exodus 10:13)   21-25-5-15-28-23-22

Israel had their first _____ before
leaving (Exodus 12:11)   31-4-2-24-41-27-40-12

22-19-29-13   31-23-38-25-36-41-19   16-6-8-8-40-7   18-41-12

26-3-2-29-10   37-13-7   4-36-39-5-32   6-22   13-9-28-19-22.

23-29   14-38-9-7,   "20-40-22   15-31   38-32-7   35-41

4-17-36-33   18-30-41-26   26-33   31-29-3-31-8-40,

21-3-22-23   33-3-15   6-13-7   22-19-40   31-29-5-31-8-29   41-18

1-24-25-36-40-8.   35-3   4-13-7   17-41-30-24-19-11-31   22-19-40

8-5-30-7,   6-10   33-3-15   23-38-27-29   2-6-9-7."

DAViD AND GOLiATH
(1 SAMUEL 17)

Across

2. Goliath's weak spot (verse 49)

5. Goliath's hometown (verse 4)

7. Long, pointy weapon (verse 7)

8. Large groups of soldiers (verse 10 SKJV)

9. Where the Philistines fled to (verse 52)

Down

1. Israel's soldiers were _____ of Goliath (verse 24)

3. He brought David to Saul (verses 55–56)

4. The position held by the man of 3 Down
    (verse 55 SKJV)

6. David's dad (verse 12)

7. David's only weapon (verse 50)

SPOTTY HEADLINE

TER●IBLE KING ●OPE●
TO KILL Y●UNG J●SUS

*Hint: There were several kings with
this name in the New Testament.*

——— ——— ——— ——— ———

WINTER SHIPWRECK!

But the **centurion**, wanting to save **Paul**, kept them from their purpose and **commanded** that those who could **swim** should cast themselves into the **sea** first and get to **land**, and the rest, some on **boards** and some on **broken** pieces of the **ship**. And so it came to pass that they all **escaped** safely to land. And when they had escaped, they then knew that the **island** was called **Malta**. And the **native** people showed us great kindness, for they **kindled** a fire and received every one of us, because of the present **rain** and because of the **cold**.

ACTS 27:43–28:2 SKJV

SPOTTY HEADLINE

PR●PHET ●UMPS SHIP,
E●TE● BY FIS●

Hint: He has a whole book of the Old Testament named for him.

___ ___ ___ ___ ___

```
Q  D  E  L  D  N  I  K  Q  K
J  B  U  P  K  N  K  N  C  T
T  A  C  K  I  L  C  O  L  D
P  T  S  A  S  H  M  I  D  N
M  H  R  E  L  M  S  R  E  E
A  S  D  R  A  O  B  U  P  K
L  R  Z  N  N  H  L  T  A  O
T  M  D  R  D  P  A  N  C  R
A  E  V  I  T  A  N  E  S  B
D  K  S  W  I  M  D  C  E  Y
```

	1	2	3	4	5
1	Y	W	H	O	S
2	P	X	B	R	L
3	K	G	I	M	A
4	N	Z	V	C	F
5	E	U	D	J	T

HEBREWS 11:1 SKJV

41-14-12 45-35-33-55-13 33-15 55-13-51

15-52-23-15-55-35-41-44-51 14-45 55-13-33-41-32-15

13-14-21-51-53 45-14-24, 55-13-51

51-43-33-53-51-41-44-51 14-45 55-13-33-41-32-15

41-14-55 15-51-51-41.

CLUES:

Canaan was promised (Genesis 17:8): L ___ ___ ___

Slow to hear and understand (Hebrews 5:11):

___ ___ ___ ___

Jacob's sneaky uncle (Genesis 29:25): L ___ ___ ___ ___

THREE BRAVE BOYS

Shadrach, **Meshach** and Abed-nego answered and said to the **king**, "O Nebuchadnezzar, we do not need to give you an **answer** to this **question**. If we are **thrown** into the **fire**, our God Whom we **serve** is able to **save** us from it. And He will save us from your hand, O king. But even if He does not, we want you to know, O king, that we will not serve your **gods** or **worship** the object of **gold** that you have **set up**."

DANIEL 3:16–18 NLV

SPOTTY HEADLINE

GO●D MAN ATTACKED
●Y ●EALOUS SATAN

Hint: Some people talk about his patience.

___ ___ ___

```
T  Q  W  O  R  S  H  I  P  H
W  U  T  A  H  S  E  T  U  P
F  E  K  I  N  G  M  Z  F  H
Z  S  W  Q  L  S  H  Q  T  C
E  T  E  T  G  C  W  H  N  A
V  I  B  V  A  O  R  E  S  R
A  O  M  H  R  O  L  D  R  D
S  N  S  L  W  E  O  D  N  A
Y  E  K  N  G  G  S  D  L  H
M  T  D  V  C  E  R  I  F  S
```

THE THREE HEBREW MEN

DANIEL 3:30 SKJV

Evil King Nebuchadnezzar wanted Shadrach,
Meshach, and Abed-nego to bow down to an idol,
but they refused. . .even when he threatened to kill them.
Crack the code to find out how their story ends!

Nebuchadnezzar's statue was sixty _____
high (Daniel 3:1 SKJV)   34-18-31-16-19-1

Regions of a nation
(Daniel 3:3 KJV)   30-22-42-39-23-10-6-20-7

The king wanted people to worship
the _____ statue (Daniel 3:7 SKJV)   40-37-28-32-21-4

The king's threat was a burning _____
furnace (Daniel 3:11 SKJV)   14-27-17-8-24

The men's names were Shadrach, _____,
and Abed-nego (Daniel 3:12)   9-26-12-35-3-15-33

The three men were brought to the _____
(Daniel 3:13)   2-25-38-29

The king saw four men in the _____ of the
fire (Daniel 3:25 SKJV)   36-11-13-5-41

19-33-20-4   41-33-21   2-27-10-40   30-8-37-9-42-41-17-13

1-35-3-32-8-3-34-33,   36-21-7-33-3-34-35,   3-38-32

3-31-21-13 - 4-26-29-42   27-38   41-33-26

30-22-37-39-11-38-6-21   37-14   31-3-31-24-28-42-10.

	1	2	3	4	5
1	P	G	E	Y	L
2	X	W	U	S	J
3	T	H	R	B	A
4	O	Q	I	F	D
5	N	C	K	M	V

1 JOHN 4:8 SKJV

32-13 22-32-41 45-41-13-24 51-41-31 15-41-55-13

45-41-13-24 51-41-31 53-51-41-22 12-41-45, 44-41-33

12-41-45 43-24 15-41-55-13.

God's Love

Across

2. It doesn't know God (1 John 3:1)

5. Caring for someone in need
   (Matthew 20:34 SKJV)

7. Love shows you have been ___ of God
   (1 John 4:7 SKJV)

8. One time God's love covers us
   (Romans 8:38 SKJV)

Down

1. Represents sinfulness in the Bible
   (Galatians 2:20 SKJV)

3. God's mercy and goodness (Isaiah 54:10 SKJV)

4. Having no end (John 3:16 NLV)

6. What Jesus' death did for us (Ephesians 2:4–5)

SPOTTY HEADLINE

EARTᗒ'S OᗒE GOOᗒD
MAN BUILDS ᗒN ARK

Hint: Really, how many guys built an ark?

___ ___ ___ ___

HOW TO THINK

Christian brothers, keep your **minds** thinking about whatever is **true**, whatever is **respected**, whatever is **right**, whatever is **pure**, whatever can be **loved**, and whatever is well **thought** of. If there is anything **good** and worth giving **thanks** for, think about these **things**. Keep on doing all the things you **learned** and received and **heard** from me. Do the things you <u>saw me do</u>. Then the **God** Who gives **peace** will be with you.

PHILIPPIANS 4:8–9 NLV

SCRAMBLED PLACE

O LOST MOVIE FUN

Hint: Jesus spent time here.

___ ___ ___ ___ ___   ___ ___

___ ___ ___ ___ ___ ___

N R D N E R V X D T
S Z I U R B C E O H
R K R G Q X N S D O
B T N Z H R S G E U
D P Y A A T D N M G
R U E E H L N I W H
A R L A O T I H A T
E E C V C K M T S H
H R E S P E C T E D
M D D O O G G O D L

THE HOLY SPIRIT ARRIVES

ACTS 2:41 SKJV

This chapter records an amazing speech by Peter. . .
as well as an amazing demonstration of God's power.
Crack the code to find out how the audience reacted!

The disciples were together on the
day of _____ (Acts 2:1 KJV)　　33-29-35-38-25-5-30-15-2

_____ of fire appeared above the
disciples (Acts 2:3)　　8-14-10-39-43-16-18

A place near Cyrene (Acts 2:10)　　41-45-6-12-23

"These men are full of _____ wine" (Acts 2:13)　　42-11-13

Whoever calls on the name of the
Lord will be _____ (Acts 2:21)　　44-17-37-9-1

Jesus' hometown (Acts 2:22)　　24-26-36-40-22-32-3-19

Jesus performed _____ and signs
(Acts 2:22 KJV)　　21-27-34-20-7-28-4-31

38-19-29-10　3-19-14-15-16　13-19-30　39-28-23-1-41-12

22-25-7-11-27-37-9-1　19-45-44　13-30-34-1　13-4-22-32

6-23-33-2-27-36-11-1,　40-35-1　3-19-4　31-17-21-32　1-26-12

23-6-14-43-2　38-19-22-25-16　3-19-30-43-44-23-35-1

31-14-43-28-15　13-11-34-11　26-1-1-16-1　3-30　8-19-29-21.

CLUES:

Farmer's storehouse (Luke 12:18): B ____ ____ ____

Where Jesus raised a widow's son

(Luke 7:11–15): ____ ____ ____ ____

Foolish husband of beautiful Abigail

(1 Samuel 25:3): N ____ ____ ____ ____

SEASONS GO ON

The **Lord** said to Himself, "I will never again **curse** the **ground** because of man. For the **desire** of man's **heart** is **sinful** from when he is **young**. I will never again **destroy** every **living** thing as I have done. While the **earth** lasts, **planting** time and gathering time, cold and heat, **summer** and **winter**, and **day** and **night** will not end."

GENESIS 8:21–22 NLV

SPOTTY HEADLINE

WOMAN ●ONO●S DEAD
H●SBAND'S MO●HER

Hint: She has a book of the Bible named for her.

___ ___ ___ ___

```
Y  N  M  M  N  S  G  W  R  L
N  O  R  D  I  P  N  I  E  H
D  M  R  N  E  E  I  N  M  E
B  A  F  T  S  S  V  T  M  A
T  U  Y  R  S  H  I  E  U  R
L  N  U  D  T  E  L  R  S  T
B  C  L  R  H  M  D  T  E  Q
L  J  A  O  G  R  O  U  N  D
F  E  P  L  A  N  T  I  N  G
T  H  G  I  N  G  N  U  O  Y
```

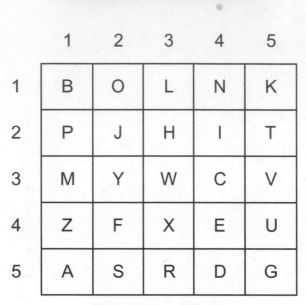

EPHESIANS 4:5 NLV

25-23-44-53-44   24-52   12-14-44   13-12-53-54   51-14-54

12-14-44   42-51-24-25-23   51-14-54   12-14-44

11-51-21-25-24-52-31.

	1	2	3	4	5
1	V	W	O	A	G
2	R	L	F	Z	D
3	J	C	B	Y	P
4	E	K	N	T	Q
5	U	H	M	S	I

JEREMIAH 29:11 NLV

"23-13-21 55 42-43-13-12 44-52-41 35-22-14-43-54

55 52-14-11-41 23-13-21 34-13-51," 54-14-34-54

44-52-41 22-13-21-25, "35-22-14-43-54 23-13-21

12-41-22-22 – 33-41-55-43-15 14-43-25 43-13-44 23-13-21

44-21-13-51-33-22-41, 44-13 15-55-11-41 34-13-51 14

23-51-44-51-21-41 14-43-25 14 52-13-35-41."

SAMSON
(Judges 13-16)

Across

1. What Samson would be (13:5)

3. He caused Manoah's wife to have a son (13:3)

6. Made from grapes (13:4)

7. She learned the secret of Samson's strength (16:18)

9. Opposite of old (15:13)

10. Sneaky animals (15:4)

Down

2. Place where Samson found a woman (14:1)

4. Tricky question (14:12 skjv)

5. Things that hold up a building (16:29)

8. Big, deadly cat (14:5)

SPOTTY HEADLINE

JEWISH B●AU●Y I● C●OSEN
QUE●N OF PE●SIA

Hint: She has a book of the Bible named for her too!

___ ___ ___ ___ ___ ___

THE END OF THE BOOK

I am **telling** everyone who hears the **words** that are **written** in this **book**: If anyone **adds** anything to what is written in this book, God will add to him the kinds of **trouble** that this book tells about. If anyone <u>takes away</u> any part of this book that tells what will **happen** in the **future**, God will take away his part from the <u>tree of life</u> and from the <u>Holy City</u>, which are told about in this book. He Who tells these things says, "Yes, I am **coming soon**!" Let it be so. Come, Lord **Jesus**. May all of you have the loving-favor of the **Lord** Jesus Christ. Let it be so.

REVELATION 22:18–21 NLV

SPOTTY HEADLINE

FIRST HUM●N ●HILD K●LLS OW● BROTHER

Hint: His name is part of a phrase for troublemaking, after the word raising.

___ ___ ___ ___

W	R	I	T	T	E	N	J	E	L
D	R	O	L	S	S	C	N	F	Y
N	B	T	O	D	A	O	G	I	A
E	L	O	R	R	D	M	N	L	W
P	N	O	O	S	D	I	I	F	A
P	W	V	U	K	S	N	L	O	S
A	N	S	R	T	B	G	L	E	E
H	E	R	U	T	U	F	E	E	K
J	E	L	B	U	O	R	T	R	A
H	O	L	Y	C	I	T	Y	T	T

PSALM 23

PSALM 23:1 SKJV

Psalm 23 is one of the most well known chapters of the Bible. Crack the code to find out how it opens!

"He leads me beside the still _____"
(Psalm 23:2 SKJV)   28-10-12-22-2-19

"The valley of the _____ of death"
(Psalm 23:4)   32-13-29-24-15-25

"You _____ a table before me"
(Psalm 23:5 SKJV)   33-6-27-31-23-21-3

Opposite of friends (Psalm 23:5 SKJV)   1-20-17-8-30-7-11

"You anoint my head with _____"
(Psalm 23:5 SKJV)   18-16-26

"All the _____ of my life" (Psalm 23:6)   4-14-9-5

12-13-27   26-15-2-4   30-32   8-9   19-13-3-33-13-1-21-24.

16   11-13-10-26-26   20-18-12   28-23-20-12.

CLUES:

His wife became a pillar of salt
(Genesis 19:15, 26): L ___ ___

There was a famous one at Babel
(Genesis 11:1–9): ___ ___ ___ ___ ___

A king or other leader (John 3:1): R ___ ___ ___ ___

ALL THINGS FOR GOOD

We **know** that God **makes** all **things** work **together** for the **good** of those who love Him and are **chosen** to be a part of <u>**His plan**</u>. God knew from the **beginning** who would put their **trust** in Him. So He chose them and made them to be like <u>**His Son**</u>. **Christ** was **first** and all those who belong to **God** are His **brothers**.

ROMANS 8:28–29 NLV

SPOTTY HEADLINE

"PROMISED L●●D" AW●ITS
●HILDRE● OF ISR●EL

Hint: Add "ites" to know who was already living there.

___ ___ ___ ___ ___ ___

```
G  Y  T  S  U  R  T  W  S  X
N  A  L  P  S  I  H  E  B  J
I  T  S  R  I  F  K  H  S  T
N  G  M  D  W  A  C  Q  R  O
N  O  O  H  M  H  H  L  E  G
I  G  S  O  O  T  R  W  H  E
G  H  J  S  D  K  I  O  T  T
E  C  E  L  I  J  S  N  O  H
B  N  B  Y  V  H  T  K  R  E
W  R  T  H  I  N  G  S  B  R
```

Jesus' Resurrection

Across

1. Day of the week Jesus rose from the dead (Mark 16:2)

3. Doubting disciple (John 20:27)

5. Number of disciples left after Jesus' death (Matthew 28:16)

7. They greeted Mary in Jesus' tomb (John 20:12)

8. They make sure nothing gets stolen (Matthew 28:4 SKJV)

Down

2. Rock covering Jesus' tomb (Luke 24:2)

3. What the women did when they heard that Jesus had risen (Mark 16:8 SKJV)

4. First of the twelve disciples to see Jesus alive (Luke 24:34)

6. Village close to Jerusalem (Luke 24:13)

SCRAMBLED PERSONS

RENT SLEEP

Hint: Only one came back to thank Jesus.

___ ___ ___   ___ ___ ___ ___ ___ ___

	1	2	3	4	5
1	N	E	H	X	L
2	R	C	P	S	A
3	Z	M	O	G	F
4	U	B	K	W	D
5	V	T	Y	J	I

JOSHUA 1:9 SKJV

"13-25-51-12 55 11-33-52 22-33-32-32-25-11-45-12-45

53-33-41? 42-12 24-52-21-33-11-34 25-11-45 33-35

34-33-33-45 22-33-41-21-25-34-12. 45-33 11-33-52 42-12

25-35-21-25-55-45 33-21 42-12 45-55-24-32-25-53-12-45,

35-33-21 52-13-12 15-33-21-45 53-33-41-21 34-33-45

55-24 44-55-52-13 53-33-41 44-13-12-21-12-51-12-21

53-33-41 34-33."

ABRAHAM AND ISAAC

GENESIS 22:12 SKJV

When God told Abraham to sacrifice his only son, Isaac, Abraham must have been scared and confused. . .but he chose to obey. Crack the code to find out what happens to Isaac!

God tested _____ (Genesis 22:1)   33-26-24-22-31-13-19

"Your only son Isaac, whom you _____"
(Genesis 22:2)   11-20-30-5

Abraham was to offer Isaac on
one of the _____ (Genesis 22:2)   17-9-6-25-8-16-2-27-32

Abraham rode a _____ with his son to
the mountain (Genesis 22:3)   28-1-38-35-10-18

Abraham prepared the burnt _____
(Genesis 22:6 KJV)   4-7-34-37-29-21-12-23

Abraham laid Isaac on the _____ of the
altar (Genesis 22:9)   36-15-14-3

13-27-3 31-5 32-33-2-28, "3-20 25-1-8 11-22-18 18-9-6-24

31-16-38-28 4-12 8-31-5 26-15-18 14-29 3-20

33-27-18-8-31-21-27-23 8-20 31-2-17, 7-4-24 38-14-36

21 35-12-20-36 8-31-16-8 18-9-6 34-10-33-29

23-9-3, 32-10-5-2-12-23 18-4-6 31-22-30-10 12-15-8

36-2-8-31-31-10-11-3 18-4-6-29 32-1-12, 18-20-6-24

4-38-11-18 32-14-27, 34-24-4-17 19-10."

YOUR HOME IN HEAVEN

"Do not let your **heart** be **troubled**. You have put your **trust** in God, put your trust in Me also. There are <u>**many rooms**</u> in My Father's **house**. If it were not so, I would have <u>**told you**</u>. I am **going** away to **make** a place for you. After I go and make a **place** for you, I will <u>**come back**</u> and take you with Me. Then you may be **where** I am. You **know** where I am going and you know how to <u>**get there**</u>."

JOHN 14:1–4 NLV

SPOTTY HEADLINE

B●AUTIFUL GAR●EN IS HUMA●S' FIRST HOM●

Hint: Where Adam and Eve lived, of course.

____ ____ ____ ____

```
M A N Y R O O M S K
H R G E T T H E R E
W O K K S R C T K T
H R U U N A J R C O
E N R S L E J O A L
R T M P E H G U B D
E K A M K O V B E Y
C B W N I W M L M O
D N O N W N V E O U
H W G L Y G Z D C B
```

THE STORY OF JONAH (JONAH 1-4)

Across

1. It swallowed Jonah (1:17)

4. Where God told Jonah to go (1:2)

6. Small, wiggly creature (4:7)

7. Jonah's dad (1:1)

9. They wrapped around Jonah's head (2:5)

Down

2. He told Jonah to pray (1:6 KJV)

3. Pumps blood, but also stands for your emotions (3:8 NLV)

5. Type of fruit (4:6 KJV)

8. Left after a fire (3:6)

SPOTTY HEADLINE

INCRE●IBLE BEIN●
W●RKS MIRACLES

Hint: They don't get any bigger or better than Him!

___ ___ ___

Cold from the North

The **storm** comes from the **south**, and the **cold** from the **north**. Water becomes **ice** by the **breath** of **God**. The wide **waters** become ice. He loads the heavy **clouds** with water and they send out His **lightning**. It changes its **path** and turns around by His **leading**, doing whatever He tells it to do on the earth where **people** live.

Job 37:9–12 NLV

SPOTTY HEADLINE

GOD CHOO●●S A N●TION
FO● H●MSE●F

Hint: It's still a nation today.

___ ___ ___ ___ ___ ___

```
W  M  C  O  L  D  M  Q  B  G
L  E  L  P  O  E  P  R  Z  N
M  S  M  X  H  C  E  N  M  I
I  H  R  T  N  A  H  M  X  N
C  P  U  E  T  O  H  R  N  T
E  O  F  H  T  T  R  O  V  H
S  Y  T  J  A  A  L  T  M  G
D  O  G  P  R  T  W  S  H  I
T  Z  C  L  O  U  D  S  W  L
G  N  I  D  A  E  L  W  G  V
```

CLUES:

Where Daniel spent a night with lions

(Daniel 6:16): D ___ ___

Can a camel go through its eye?

(Mark 10:25): ___ ___ ___ ___ ___ ___

Adam and Eve's garden (Genesis 2:15): E ___ ___ ___

God CALLS SAMUEL

1 SAMUEL 3:19 NLV

When God called Samuel, Samuel didn't know
what was going on. Crack the code to see
what became of Samuel's life after this.

At this time, Samuel was just a _____
(1 Samuel 3:1 KJV)   9-28-19-1-13

Samuel _____ to the Lord before
Eli (1 Samuel 3:1 KJV)   4-15-12-29-10-31-6-33-11-24

The _____ of the Lord wasn't revealed to
Samuel yet (1 Samuel 3:7)   5-18-16-14

Samuel called himself the Lord's _____
(1 Samuel 3:10)   35-27-23-8-2-36-3

Samuel waited until _____ to tell Eli the
vision (1 Samuel 3:15)   20-17-30-21-34-26-7

"What did the Lord tell _____?"
(1 Samuel 3:17 NLV)   22-32-25

10-2-20-25-6-1   7-16-11-5.   2-12-13   31-28-27   1-18-33-24

5-2-35   5-15-3-28   28-19-20   2-36-14   20-2-13-27

11-8-27-23-22-3-28-29-21-7   28-6   35-2-19-14   9-17-20-27

31-16-25-11.

JESUS' BIRTH

Across

1. How long Jesus' kingdom will last (Luke 1:33 KJV)

3. Where the wise men saw Jesus' star (Matthew 2:2)

7. What the wise men did when they found Jesus (Matthew 2:11 NLV)

8. Angry King Herod wanted to _____ young Jesus (Matthew 2:16 NLV)

9. A place where you stay the night (Luke 2:7 KJV)

Down

2. What God offers (Luke 2:38 KJV)

4. The kind of clothes baby Jesus had (Luke 2:12 KJV)

5. A mighty angel (Luke 1:26)

6. Old Testament wife of Jacob (Matthew 2:18)

SPOTTY HEADLINE

BROTH●R OF ●OHN IS FIR●T ●●RTYR

Hint: There's also a book of the New Testament by this name—but by a different author.

____ ____ ____ ____ ____

INSTRUCTIONS FOR TITUS

To **Titus**, my own son after the common **faith**: **grace**, **mercy**, and **peace** from God the **Father** and the Lord **Jesus** Christ our **Savior**. For this reason I left you in **Crete**, that you should set in **order** the things that are lacking and ordain **elders** in every city, as I had appointed you, if anyone is **blameless**, the husband of one wife, having faithful **children** not accused of riot or unruly.
TITUS 1:4–6 SKJV

SPOTTY HEADLINE

CAR●ENT●R IS ●ESU●' F●STER FAT●ER

Hint: A kid with a "coat of many colors" also had this name.

___ ___ ___ ___ ___ ___

```
T  B  P  C  R  T  S  D  E  T
M  K  L  E  R  Q  U  L  T  P
N  E  D  A  H  O  T  G  E  E
R  R  R  T  M  F  I  B  R  A
O  N  I  C  A  E  T  V  C  C
B  A  R  T  Y  J  L  G  A  E
F  Z  H  G  R  A  C  E  Y  S
C  E  S  U  S  E  J  B  S  N
R  Z  L  E  L  D  E  R  S  S
C  H  I  L  D  R  E  N  T  V
```

	1	2	3	4	5
1	T	E	Z	A	S
2	N	G	X	F	U
3	R	I	B	D	J
4	Y	C	P	K	W
5	H	V	L	M	O

PSALM 119:105 NLV

41-55-25-31 45-55-31-34 32-15 14 53-14-54-43 11-55

54-41 24-12-12-11 14-21-34 14 53-32-22-51-11 11-55 54-41

43-14-11-51.

CLUES:

God's rules and commands, all together

(Deuteronomy 4:44): L ___ ___

Life-giving liquid (John 4:14): ___ ___ ___ ___ ___

Help and comfort in trouble

(Acts 11:29): R ___ ___ ___ ___ ___

God Creates a Woman

And the **Lord God** caused a deep **sleep** to fall on **Adam**, and he slept. And He took one of his **ribs** and <u>**closed up**</u> the **flesh** instead of it. And from the rib, which the Lord God had taken from man, He **made** a **woman** and **brought** her to the man. And Adam said, "This is now **bone** of my bones and flesh of my flesh; <u>**she shall**</u> be **called** Woman, because she was **taken** out of Man."

Genesis 2:21–23 SKJV

SPOTTY HEADLINE

MO●ES' HELPER ●OINS ●IM ●N MO●NT SIN●I

Hint: He defeated Jericho.

___ ___ ___ ___ ___ ___

```
D  L  E  D  A  M  Q  P  M  L
O  T  X  C  D  D  E  R  F  N
G  H  N  L  A  E  W  E  B  C
D  G  T  A  L  L  N  B  F  L
R  U  A  S  M  O  L  L  L  O
O  O  K  R  B  O  E  E  L  S
L  R  E  R  I  S  W  C  D  E
M  B  N  R  H  B  P  N  C  D
B  A  D  A  M  F  S  X  M  U
G  S  H  E  S  H  A  L  L  P
```

HeZeKiAH'S MIRACULOUS GIFT

ISAIAH 38:20 NLV

Hezekiah was sick and about to die. . .but a simple prayer changed everything. Crack the code to find out how Hezekiah reacted to God's mercy.

Isaiah was a _____ (Isaiah 38:1 KJV)   11-4-3-10-39-16-12

Eagerly; with all you have
(Isaiah 38:3 SKJV)   24-42-31-1-35-13-38-32-45-7-28-33-6-29

Measures the time of day
(Isaiah 38:8 SKJV)   40-2-27-21-23-36-20

At the halfway mark
(Isaiah 38:10 SKJV)   43-17-14-26-34-19

"For the _____ cannot praise You"
(Isaiah 38:18 SKJV)   37-30-44-15-8

Tells his children about God's truth
(Isaiah 38:19)   18-5-41-22-25-9

"12-42-16   20-3-45-33   24-23-34-1   40-32-15-25   43-8.

36-27-14   24-28   24-17-6-1   40-23-27-37   43-29

40-31-27-37-40   24-23-7-42   13-32-4-11-40   32-20-1   12-13-19

26-5-29-40   3-18   31-2-30   34-17-18-35   17-27   41-22-16

39-3-2-40-8   31-18   41-42-19   20-3-30-33."

	1	2	3	4	5
1	D	X	R	G	Y
2	P	N	B	Z	H
3	E	S	I	F	M
4	A	T	O	U	J
5	W	L	V	C	K

MATTHEW 5:6 SKJV

23-52-31-32-32-31-11 41-13-31 42-25-43-32-31 51-25-43

25-44-22-14-31-13 41-22-11 42-25-33-13-32-42

41-34-42-31-13 13-33-14-25-42-31-43-44-32-22-31-32-32,

34-43-13 42-25-31-15 32-25-41-52-52 23-31

34-33-52-52-31-11.

FoRgiveNess

Across

1. Money you owe (Matthew 6:12 KJV)

7. Disobeyed; fought back (Daniel 9:9 KJV)

8. When you think of the past (Isaiah 43:25)

9. We should forgive _____ times seven times! (Matthew 18:22)

Down

2. When you hold a grudge (Ephesians 4:31 KJV)

3. What God shows to us (Proverbs 28:13 SKJV)

4. Bad intentions (Ephesians 4:31 KJV)

5. Color God uses to describe sin (Isaiah 1:18 NLV)

6. Who Jesus asked to forgive His killers (Luke 23:34)

SCRAMBLED PLACE

A CURL MOMENT

Hint: Think Elijah and the prophets of Baal.

___ ___ ___ ___ ___

___ ___ ___ ___ ___ ___

SUMMER AND WINTER ARE BOTH GOD'S

It was You Who **opened** up the earth for **water** to **flow out**. And You **dried** up **rivers** that flow forever. The **day** is Yours. And the **night** is Yours. You have set the **light** and the **sun** in their **places**. You have divided all the **lands** and seas and nations of the earth. You have made **summer** and **winter**.

PSALM 74:15–17 NLV

SPOTTY HEADLINE

●ESUS' BROTH●R WRITES
●OWN TR●TH

Hint: It's the name of a one-chapter book of the New Testament.

____ ____ ____ ____

```
W   A   T   E   R   Y   R   R   T   P
F   Y   A   D   Q   I   U   E   M   L
T   L   R   S   V   H   O   T   R   V
H   T   O   E   D   D   Y   N   L   J
G   T   R   W   E   N   S   I   D   S
I   S   H   N   O   H   A   W   R   U
L   P   E   G   Q   U   W   L   I   M
K   P   N   M   I   J   T   N   E   M
O   U   W   R   H   N   I   N   D   E
S   F   P   L   A   C   E   S   T   R
```

THE TEN COMMANDMENTS
(EXODUS 20:1-17)

Across

1. Another word for slavery (verse 2 KJV)

7. Where God lives (verse 4)

8. Obey your parents for a ___ life (verse 12)

9. God's holy day (verse 8 KJV)

10. Planet full of life (verse 4)

Down

2. Carved or engraved (verse 4 KJV)

3. Don't want this animal that belongs to someone else (verse 17 NLV)

4. A person who lives nearby (verse 16 NLV)

5. Not true (verse 16 KJV)

6. What God does to evil (verse 7 NLV)

SPOTTY HEADLINE

MAN'S WIFE ●URNS INT●
PIL●AR OF SALT!

Hint: He was Abraham's nephew.

___ ___ ___

CAPTAIN OF THE LORD'S ARMY

And it came to pass, when **Joshua** was by **Jericho**, that he lifted up his **eyes** and looked, and, **behold**, a man stood across from him with his **sword** drawn in his hand. And Joshua went to him and said to him, "Are you <u>**for us**</u> or for our adversaries?" And he said, "No, but as **captain** of the army of the LORD, I have now come." And Joshua **fell** on his **face** to the **earth** and **worshipped**, and said to him, "What does my lord say to his **servant**?"

JOSHUA 5:13–14 SKJV

SPOTTY HEADLINE

MEDICA● MAN S●RVIV●S SHIPWREC●

Hint: He wrote one of the four Gospels.

—— —— ——

```
W   O   R   S   H   I   P   P   E   D
H   S   E   R   V   A   N   T   A   S
N   I   A   T   P   A   C   T   U   W
B   D   E   Y   E   S   W   O   H   O
L   E   K   Y   M   V   H   H   S   R
L   F   H   X   F   C   D   E   O   D
E   R   B   O   I   G   C   R   J   Y
F   M   R   R   L   A   M   L   O   F
T   U   E   M   F   D   T   R   R   L
S   J   E   A   R   T   H   L   Z   L
```

CLUES:

Make better in body, mind, or spirit (Psalm 6:2):

H ____ ____ ____

To a smaller extent (Exodus 16:17): ____ ____ ____ ____

Bottom of a foot (2 Samuel 14:25): S ____ ____ ____

THE "ROMANS ROAD"

ROMANS 10:13 NLV

Romans 10 is a beautiful chapter about God's grace. Crack the code for a short summary of how a person can be saved.

Paul wanted _____ to be saved
(Romans 10:1 KJV)   29-25-43-30-41-14

A conversation with God
(Romans 10:1 KJV)   44-12-39-46-31-40

For Christians, _____ is the end of the
law (Romans 10:4)   23-4-21-33-6-34

The man who follows the law shall _____
by it (Romans 10:5)   15-26-17-45

"How shall they believe in Him of _____
they have not heard?"   (Romans 10:14 SKJV) 18-24-3-38

The feet of Gospel-preachers
are _____ (Romans 10:15)   9-8-35-2-7-32-20-36-37

Rebellious
(Romans 10:21 KJV)   10-13-16-5-11-1-28-27-22-19-42

20-3-40   8-17-22-40-46-5-19-41   18-4-5   23-30-15-37-6

3-19   34-24-31   19-39-38-1   3-20   42-24-8   37-3-43-10

18-33-14-15   11-31   16-39-17-41-28   20-21-5-38   34-4-8

44-2-19-32-6-4-38-41-19-7   5-20   6-26-19.

THE WALLS OF JERICHO (JOSHUA 6)

Across

2. How the Israelites shouted (verse 5 NLV)

5. Opposite of blessed (verse 18 KJV)

7. How Jericho's walls ended up (verse 20 SKJV)

8. Days the people marched around the city (verse 4)

10. God's chosen nation (verse 1)

Down

1. She was spared by Joshua's army (verse 25)

3. How Jericho was destroyed (verse 21 KJV)

4. A loud instrument (verse 5 KJV)

6. What the people did in tents (verse 11 NLV)

9. Sharp part of a sword (verse 21 KJV)

SPOTTY HEADLINE

YOUNG ●AN ●UNS NA●ED
FROM JESUS' ●RREST

Hint: He also wrote one of the four Gospels!

_____ _____ _____ _____

JESUS AND THE SAMARITAN WOMAN

The **woman** left her <u>**water jar**</u> and went into the **town**. She said to the men, "<u>**Come and see**</u> a Man Who told me everything I ever did! Can this be the **Christ**?" They went out of town and came to Him. . . . Many people in that town of **Samaria believed** in Jesus because of what the woman said about Him. She said, "He **told** me **everything** I ever did." So the **people** of Samaria came to Him. They asked Him to **stay** with them. Jesus stayed there <u>**two days**</u>.
JOHN 4:28–30, 39–40 NLV

SCRAMBLED EVENT

PUTS PEARLS

Hint: Jesus had this with His disciples.

___ ___ ___ ___   ___ ___ ___ ___ ___ ___

```
G  C  D  E  V  E  I  L  E  B
N  O  T  W  O  D  A  Y  S  N
I  M  T  O  W  N  R  A  F  R
H  E  T  H  G  V  M  N  A  P
T  A  C  G  B  A  N  J  L  E
Y  N  Q  H  R  K  R  Y  N  O
R  D  D  I  R  E  R  Y  A  P
E  S  A  L  T  I  A  Y  M  L
V  E  H  A  O  T  S  T  O  E
E  E  W  F  S  T  B  T  W  C
```

Jesus' First Days
(Luke 2)

Across

3. "_____ on earth" (verse 14)

5. He led Simeon to see Jesus (verse 27 KJV)

6. Set apart for God (verse 23)

8. A messenger from God (verse 9)

9. Jesus' early hometown (verse 39)

Down

1. A count demanded by Caesar (verse 1 SKJV)

2. Where the Jews went to worship God (verse 27 KJV)

4. City of David (verse 4)

7. Very old woman of God in Jerusalem (verse 36)

SPOTTY HEADLINE

●ARY'S SIS●ER FRUSTR●TED
BY ●LL ●ER WO●K

Hint: She was also a sister of Lazarus.

—— —— —— —— —— ——

GIVING LIFE,
GETTING LIFE

Jesus said to His **followers**, "If anyone wants to be My follower, he must **forget** about himself. He must take up his **cross** and follow Me. If **anyone** wants to **keep** his **life** safe, he will lose it. If anyone **gives up** his life because of Me, he will **save** it. For what does a man have if he gets all the **world** and loses his own **soul**? What can a man give to **buy back** his soul?"
MATTHEW 16:24–26 NLV

SPOTTY HEADLINE

●OSES' SISTE● ●OVES ●ND
SINGS ●N CELEBRAT●ON

Hint: Her name is a form of Mary.

___ ___ ___ ___ ___

```
B  U  Y  B  A  C  K  K  S  C
H  K  L  N  F  Q  E  R  U  H
T  C  N  B  L  E  E  N  S  T
D  B  R  U  P  W  A  G  E  K
L  E  O  O  O  L  N  I  J  D
R  S  V  L  S  Q  Y  V  W  T
O  L  L  A  Z  S  O  E  H  N
W  O  N  M  S  R  N  S  W  G
F  O  R  G  E  T  E  U  K  N
F  E  F  I  L  T  J  P  W  Y
```

CLUES:

Joseph's brothers threw him into one

(Genesis 37:24): P ____ ____

Missionary companion of Paul (Galatians 2:1):

____ ____ ____ ____ ____

Jesus had a "last" one with His disciples

(Luke 22:20): S ____ ____ ____ ____ ____

NEHEMIAH'S WALL
NEHEMIAH 6:15 NLV

Nehemiah's dream was to rebuild Jerusalem's walls. . .but his enemies had other plans. Crack the code to find out if he succeeded!

Went without eating (Nehemiah 1:4 KJV)

24-13-23-10-17-3

Nehemiah to the king: "Why _____ my face not be sad?" (Nehemiah 2:3)

8-11-25-2-21-20

The people had a _____ to work (Nehemiah 4:6)

12-9-14-19

"Why should the work stop while I. . . come down to _____?" (Nehemiah 6:3 NLV)

5-22-1

Shemaiah wanted to meet Nehemiah _____ the temple (Nehemiah 6:10 KJV)

7-16-4-18-6-15

23-25 4-11-17 7-13-21-21 7-13-8 24-16-15-9-23-11-17-3

22-14 10-18-17 10-7-17-15-4-5 – 24-6-24-4-11 19-13-5

22-24 4-18-17 12-22-14-10-11 22-24 17-21-1-21, 9-15

24-16-24-4-5 – 10-7-25 20-13-5-23.

Jesus' Miracles

Across

4. Unable to talk (Matthew 9:32 SKJV)

6. Where Jesus' first miracle happened (John 2:1)

7. A bad skin disease (Mark 1:42 KJV)

9. Pool where a blind man washed (John 9:7)

10. Where Jesus raised a widow's son to life
    (Luke 7:11)

Down

1. What Jesus did for sick people (Mark 10:45 NLV)

2. Evil spirit thrown out by Jesus (Matthew 12:22)

3. A word Jesus used for "death" (John 11:11)

5. Number of years one woman was sick
   (Luke 13:11)

8. Where four men lowered their sick friend to Jesus
   (Mark 2:4)

SPOTTY HEADLINE

SLAVER● NA●ION
SLAMM●D BY ●LA●UES

Hint: It's still a nation today.

___ ___ ___ ___ ___

WINTER IN CORINTH

Now I will come to you when I pass through **Macedonia**, for I am passing through Macedonia. And it may be that I will **remain**, yes, and **spend** the **winter** with you, that you may **send** me on my **journey**, wherever I go. For I will not see you now <u>on the way</u>, but I trust to remain with you a while, if the **Lord permits**. But I will remain at **Ephesus** until **Pentecost**, for a great and effective **door** has **opened** to me, and there are many adversaries.

1 CORINTHIANS 16:5–9 SKJV

SPOTTY HEADLINE

W●TER PA●TS TO L●T GO●'● PEOPL● THROUGH!

Hint: A colorful ocean.

___ ___ ___   ___ ___ ___

```
O  S  L  C  W  A  N  P  K  V
P  E  R  L  L  I  O  E  S  S
E  N  R  O  A  N  N  N  U  T
N  D  R  M  O  O  T  T  S  I
E  D  E  Q  F  D  H  E  E  M
D  R  Z  L  N  E  E  C  H  R
S  P  E  N  D  C  W  O  P  E
J  N  B  W  T  A  A  S  E  P
R  F  M  Q  K  M  Y  T  N  R
P  Y  E  N  R  U  O  J  K  N
```

PAUL'S TRIP TO ROME (ACTS 27-28)

Across

3. Snowy season (27:12)

5. Leader of a hundred Roman soldiers (27:6 KJV)

8. Slithery surprise (28:3 NLV)

Down

1. Number of years Paul stayed in Rome (28:30)

2. The heat you feel when you're sick (28:8)

4. Used to hold a ship down (27:30)

5. Paul and other prisoners wore these (27:42 NLV)

6. Number of months Paul spent on Malta (28:11)

7. Old Testament prophet Paul quoted (28:25)

SPOTTY HEADLINE

●OOR LE●DER A●LOWS J●SUS ●O D●E

Hint: He did not fly airplanes.

___ ___ ___ ___ ___ ___

PRide IS TROUBLE

The vision of **Obadiah**. This is what the <u>Lord God</u> says concerning **Edom**: (We have heard a **rumor** from the Lord, and an ambassador was sent among the **nations**, saying, "**Arise**, and let us rise up against her in **battle**.") "Behold, I have made you **small** among the nations. You are greatly despised. The **pride** of your **heart** has deceived you, you who dwell in the **clefts** of the **rock**, whose habitation is high, who say in your heart, 'Who shall bring me down to the **ground**?' "
OBADIAH 1–3 SKJV

SPOTTY HEADLINE

STRONG M●N HA●
WEAKNE●S FOR WO●E●

Hint: Delilah cut off his hair.

___ ___ ___ ___ ___ ___

M	J	F	M	E	L	T	T	A	B
E	H	G	L	M	Y	A	N	D	H
D	A	J	B	L	R	W	O	B	D
I	I	G	K	I	A	G	H	N	H
R	D	R	S	R	D	M	U	A	E
P	A	E	U	R	O	O	S	T	A
R	B	W	O	M	R	C	Q	I	R
C	O	L	N	G	O	B	K	O	T
S	T	F	E	L	C	R	X	N	B
R	K	E	D	O	M	R	D	S	M

CLUES:

Eve was this to Adam (Genesis 2:18): H ____ ____ ____

Ruler of Egypt (Exodus 3:10): ____ ____ ____ ____ ____ ____

Where the leg bones connect (Judges 15:8): H ____ ____

GOD'S CONVERSATION WITH JOB

JOB 42:10 SKJV

Job didn't understand why God allowed bad
things to happen to him. . .but God later stepped
in to set everything straight. Crack the code to
see how Job was rewarded for his faithfulness!

God spoke to Job out of a _____
(Job 38:1 KJV)   7-17-43-6-4-32-16-27-29

Essential for strong buildings
(Job 38:4 SKJV)   3-39-11-8-30-26-28-2-19-1-25

"Will you hunt the _____ for the lion?"
(Job 38:39 KJV)   13-45-10-15

God's _____ is always right
(Job 40:8 KJV)   36-34-21-44-40-23-42-24

An important agreement
(Job 41:4 KJV)   9-12-37-14-35-41-18-22

"My anger _____ against you and your
two friends" (Job 42:7 NLV)   31-20-33-5-38

41-27-30   28-17-10   4-39-45-21   24-11-33-1-23-29

22-17-14   9-26-13-24-43-37-2-28-15   19-3   36-12-31

7-17-10-35   17-23   13-33-26-15-14-30   3-12-45   17-2-25

3-6-16-10-18-29-38.   41-4-25-39   24-17-23   4-12-6-30

44-41-37-23   36-12-31   24-32-16-9-10   41-25

40-20-9-17   26-38   17-23   17-41-21   31-10-3-12-33-14.

REPENTANCE

Across

1. What God has done for all His children (Acts 8:22 KJV)

5. Where Saul was headed when Jesus stopped him (Acts 9:2)

7. Go back (Zechariah 1:3)

8. The Ninevites' response to Jonah's message (Jonah 3:5)

Down

1. No longer missing (Luke 15:24)

2. People who disobey God (Luke 5:32)

3. Our sure hope as Christians (Matthew 4:17)

4. The tree Zacchaeus climbed before he met Jesus (Luke 19:4 NLV)

6. How we should feel over sin (2 Peter 3:9 NLV)

SCRAMBLED THING

UH BRING BUNS

Hint: It talked to Moses.

___ ___ ___ ___ ___ ___ ___

___ ___ ___ ___

WHAT IS FAITH?

Now **faith** is **being sure** we will get what we **hope** for. It is being sure of what we **cannot see**. **God** was **pleased** with the **men** who had faith who lived long ago. Through faith we **understand** that the **world** was made by the **Word of God**. Things we see were **made** from what could not be **seen**.

HEBREWS 11:1–3 NLV

SPOTTY HEADLINE

JESUS CHA●GED TH●S MAN'● NA●E T● PETER

Hint: The name also belonged to a tanner, a leper, and a magician.

___ ___ ___ ___ ___

J	W	O	R	D	O	F	G	O	D
N	C	D	L	G	R	N	C	F	N
S	U	R	E	N	I	J	A	H	A
H	O	N	N	E	E	S	N	T	T
W	O	B	B	K	H	M	N	I	S
L	N	P	G	K	K	V	O	A	R
V	T	O	E	M	L	F	T	F	E
M	D	C	F	L	A	V	S	C	D
M	C	Y	F	Y	G	D	E	N	N
D	E	S	A	E	L	P	E	N	U

MOSES LEADS THE ISRAELITES OUT OF EGYPT (EXODUS 3-14)

Across

4. Used in making bricks (5:7)

5. The Red Sea bottom as the Israelites walked through (14:29)

9. What the waters of Egypt became (7:19)

10. His walking stick became a snake (7:10)

Down

1. The Israelites' promised land flowed with this (3:8)

2. What God spoke to Moses from (3:4)

3. They died in the final plague (11:5)

6. Another word for "walking stick" (7:17 KJV)

7. He spoke to Pharaoh (6:10–11)

8. What the Israelites shouldn't do (14:13 KJV)

177

PRESS ON

Not as though I had **already** attained, or were already **perfect**, but I **follow** after, if that I may apprehend that for which also I am apprehended of **Christ** Jesus. Brothers, I do not **count** myself to have apprehended, but this one thing I do, **forgetting** those things that are **behind** and reaching **forward** to those things that are **ahead**, I **press** toward the **mark** for the **prize** of the high calling of God in Christ **Jesus**.
PHILIPPIANS 3:12–14 SKJV

SPOTTY HEADLINE

ENO●MOUS BO●T IS PAC●ED WITH ANIMALS

Hint: It was Noah's, of course.

—— —— ——

N	P	R	I	Z	E	T	R	G	D
C	H	S	W	X	C	N	P	N	D
O	J	K	S	E	K	Q	V	I	R
U	M	E	F	E	B	J	Y	T	A
N	C	R	S	E	R	K	D	T	W
T	E	H	H	U	R	P	A	E	R
P	M	I	R	A	S	F	E	G	O
L	N	P	M	I	T	F	R	R	F
D	A	E	H	A	S	V	L	O	T
F	O	L	L	O	W	T	A	F	N

CLUES:

Another name for birds in general

(Genesis 1:20): F ____ ____ ____

What the dove brought back to Noah

(Genesis 8:11): ____ ____ ____ ____

Silly, bad choices (Proverbs 5:23): F ____ ____ ____ ____

	1	2	3	4	5
1	K	W	Q	A	Z
2	R	T	I	P	L
3	F	O	G	M	H
4	Y	E	U	V	C
5	D	N	J	B	S

2 CORINTHIANS 5:17 SKJV

22-35-42-21-42-31-32-21-42 23-31 14-52-41 34-14-52 23-55

23-52 45-35-21-23-55-22, 35-42 23-55 14

52-42-12 45-21-42-14-22-43-21-42. 32-25-51

22-35-23-52-33-55 35-14-44-42 24-14-55-55-42-51

14-12-14-41; 54-42-35-32-25-51, 14-25-25

22-35-23-52-33-55 35-14-44-42 54-42-45-32-34-42

52-42-12.

HEAVEN

Across

2. Color of clothes in heaven (Revelation 3:5)

4. Christians' names are _____ in heaven (Luke 10:20)

6. God's seat (Revelation 3:21)

8. Direction of heaven (Colossians 3:2 KJV)

9. Jesus gave Peter the ___ to the kingdom of heaven (Matthew 16:18–19)

Down

1. Jesus said the kingdom of heaven is made up of people like this (Matthew 19:14)

3. Heaven is not made by these (2 Corinthians 5:1)

5. People who live in a country (Philippians 3:20 NLV)

7. How far away the kingdom of heaven is (Matthew 4:17 NLV)

SPOTTY HEADLINE

●URIAL CAVE IS ●ISSING
●HE B●DY OF JESUS!

Hint: Another word for "grave."

___ ___ ___ ___

WHEN PAUL GOT COLD

I have made many **hard** trips. I have been in **danger** from high water on **rivers**. I have been in danger from **robbers**. I have been in danger from the Jews. I have been in danger from **people** who do not know God. I have been in danger in **cities** and in the **desert**. I have been in danger on the sea. I have been in danger among people who say they belong to **Christ** but do not. I have **worked** hard and have been tired and have had **pain**. I have gone many times without **sleep**. I have been **hungry** and thirsty. I have gone without food and **clothes**. I have been out in the **cold**.

2 CORINTHIANS 11:26–27 NLV

SPOTTY HEADLINE

●ARGE CAT● ●OT
HUNGRY F●R DAN●EL

Hint: Some call them "king of the jungle."

— — — — — —

```
C  R  R  I  V  E  R  S  R  T
P  C  O  N  I  A  P  E  T  K
P  H  P  B  Y  R  G  N  U  H
E  R  E  C  B  N  W  J  K  N
O  I  E  L  A  E  O  M  S  D
P  S  L  D  D  N  R  N  E  G
L  T  S  L  R  X  K  S  I  Z
E  F  O  K  A  X  E  B  T  N
R  C  N  K  H  R  D  B  I  M
T  S  E  H  T  O  L  C  C  L
```

SOLOMON'S FAME

1 KINGS 11:4 SKJV

God gifted Solomon with tons of wisdom and riches. . .but Solomon eventually started wasting these gifts on sinful activities. Crack the code to find out what led to his downfall.

All Israel saw Solomon's _____
(1 Kings 3:28)   6-32-37-27-30-31

Hiram was the king of _____ (1 Kings 5:1)   1-19-17-28

By the ocean (1 Kings 4:29 KJV)   39-7-36-23-35-15-13-20

Solomon's temple had the _____ of
Judgment (1 Kings 7:7 KJV)   12-24-26-22-34

God _____ His promise to David
(1 Kings 8:24 KJV)   14-9-3-16-4-38-5-18-21

More valuable than silver (1 Kings 10:2)   8-11-10-25

A fleet of ships (1 Kings 10:11 KJV)   2-29-33-40

14-30-13 32-1 22-36-31-7 1-15 12-36-37-39, 6-35-28-2

23-24-10-11-31-30-2 6-36-37 15-10-27, 1-34-36-1 35-32-39

6-4-33-7-37 1-9-13-2-28-25 36-6-29-19 34-4-37

35-20-36-26-1 36-14-1-28-13 24-1-35-18-17 8-30-25-39.

36-2-21 35-4-39 35-20-36-26-1 6-36-37 2-11-1

12-7-17-14-28-22-1 6-32-1-35 1-34-7 38-11-26-27 34-4-39

8-24-27, 36-37 6-36-39 1-34-7 34-28-36-17-1 24-14

34-32-39 14-36-1-34-7-26, 21-36-33-32-25.

CLUES:

Not alive (Romans 7:11): D ___ ___ ___

Something you do (Acts 4:9): ___ ___ ___ ___

A king's announcement (Luke 2:1):

D ___ ___ ___ ___ ___

SALVATION

Across

1. These are *not* what saves us (Titus 3:5 KJV)

3. Strong trust (Ephesians 2:8)

5. What can't be done (Luke 18:27 KJV)

8. Where belief happens (Romans 10:9)

Down

1. What a patient person does (Psalm 62:1)

2. What sin makes us (John 3:18 NLV)

4. Amount of people who have sinned (Romans 3:23)

6. Rescued; freed from sin (Acts 16:31)

7. To speak to God (Hebrews 7:25 NLV)

SPOTTY HEADLINE

JOSUS' ●IR●●P●ACE
PROP●ESIED ●ANY
Y●ARS B●FORE

Hint: We sing of the "little town" at Christmastime.

___ ___ ___ ___ ___ ___ ___ ___ ___

JESUS' REAL FAMILY

Then His **mother** and **brothers** came and **stood** outside.
They sent for **Jesus**. Many people were **sitting** around Him.
They said, "See! Your mother and brothers are **outside**
looking for You." He said to them, "Who is My mother or My
brothers?" He turned to those sitting around Him and said,
"**See!** My mother and My brothers! **Whoever** does what My
Father wants is My brother and My **sister** and My mother."

MARK 3:31–35 NLV

SCRAMBLED PERSON

FOURTH JAGUAR DIES

Hint: Jesus brought her back to life!

__ __ __ __ __ __ __ __

__ __   __ __ __ __ __ __

R	T	S	T	O	O	D	L	D	R
J	F	A	T	H	E	R	S	S	E
J	E	C	G	S	R	R	Z	I	V
R	T	S	T	B	E	M	O	T	E
Q	J	N	U	H	H	U	L	T	O
H	A	Q	T	S	T	T	Z	I	H
W	Z	O	P	S	O	F	N	N	W
E	R	R	I	Q	M	R	R	G	L
B	E	D	G	N	I	K	O	O	L
B	E	S	R	E	T	S	I	S	M

191

	1	2	3	4	5
1	P	M	D	L	I
2	N	A	B	E	F
3	O	C	G	T	K
4	Y	V	S	R	J
5	U	Z	W	H	X

JOB 38:4 SKJV

"53-54-24-44-24 53-24-44-24 41-31-51

53-54-24-21 15 14-22-15-13 34-54-24

25-31-51-21-13-22-34-15-31-21-43 31-25 34-54-24

24-22-44-34-54? 13-24-32-14-22-44-24, 15-25 41-31-51

54-22-42-24 51-21-13-24-44-43-34-22-21-13-15-21-33."

GideoN

JUDGES 7:22 SKJV

God called Gideon to defeat a vast army. . .and his
men didn't even have to fight. Crack the code to
find out how God pulled off this impossible feat!

Israel was oppressed by the _____
(Judges 6:3 KJV)   13-3-15-8-5-11-19-28-25-24

Gideon was a "mighty man of _____"
(Judges 6:12 SKJV)   29-31-7-33-6

God had delivered Israel from _____
(Judges 6:13)   22-4-9-14-10

Usually found on the grass in the morning
(Judges 6:37 KJV)   2-12-34

Three _____ men remained in Gideon's
army (Judges 7:6)   27-21-16-17-35-23-20

Most of Gideon's men _____ to drink water
(Judges 7:6 KJV)   1-18-32-30-26

5-11-17   28-27-25   10-27-35-22-23   27-21-11-15-6-12-26

1-7-30-34   28-27-22   28-35-21-13-14-30-10-24,   5-16-26

10-27-25   7-33-35-15   24-22-28   23-29-12-6-9   13-31-11-'24

24-32-33-35-26   31-4-5-3-11-24-10   18-11-23

31-11-33-28-27-30-6   10-27-35-33-21-4-27-18-21-10   31-7-7

10-27-25   5-6-13-9.

Jesus' Sermon on the Mount (Matthew 5–7)

Across

1. Where farmers store grain (6:26 KJV)

3. A tiny grain of something (7:3 SKJV)

6. When a marriage ends (5:32 NLV)

7. Helps you see in the dark (5:15 KJV)

Down

1. What God's children are (5:3 KJV)

2. Preserves food and makes it taste better (5:13)

3. A poor foundation (7:26)

4. To look down on someone (7:1 KJV)

5. Someone who doesn't follow good advice (5:22)

SPOTTY HEADLINE

BIBLI●A● "TRUCK" H●S
FOUR F●ET AND HU●P

Hint: Jesus talked about this going through the eye of a needle.

___ ___ ___ ___ ___

keep YouRSelf iN God'S love

But you, **beloved**, building up yourselves on your most <u>**holy**</u> <u>**faith**</u>, praying in the **Holy Spirit**, **keep** yourselves in the <u>**love of God**</u>, looking for the **mercy** of our Lord **Jesus** Christ to **eternal** life. And on some have compassion, making a difference, and others **save** with **fear**, pulling them out of the **fire**, hating even the **garment** stained by the **flesh**.

JUDE 20–23 SKJV

SPOTTY HEADLINE

NAME DES●●IBES JESUS' M●SSION A● ●HE MESSIA●

Hint: It often follows the name Jesus.

—— —— —— —— —— ——

```
G  A  R  M  E  N  T  M  H  N
Q  L  L  P  R  V  E  T  O  R
M  O  F  B  K  R  A  E  L  A
T  V  D  R  C  E  R  S  Y  E
F  E  E  Y  J  I  E  G  F  F
L  O  V  R  F  D  M  P  A  K
E  F  O  Y  S  P  I  R  I  T
S  G  L  L  A  N  R  E  T  E
H  O  E  M  W  X  M  K  H  V
H  D  B  G  Z  S  U  S  E  J
```

CLUES:

Purple or scarlet, for example (Revelation 17:4):

C ____ ____ ____ ____

What happened to the stone over Jesus' tomb

(Matthew 28:2): ____ ____ ____ ____ ____ ____

Jesus called Himself this "of the sheep"

(John 10:7): D ____ ____ ____

	1	2	3	4	5
1	Y	Z	A	K	W
2	O	N	F	P	S
3	J	E	U	H	X
4	C	I	R	M	V
5	G	D	B	T	L

PSALM 23:1 NLV

54-34-32 55-21-43-52 42-25 44-11

25-34-32-24-34-32-43-52. 42 15-42-55-55

34-13-45-32 32-45-32-43-11-54-34-42-22-51 42

22-32-32-52.

ESTHER'S AMAZING COURAGE (ESTHER 1-10)

Across

1. Used to make people smell good (2:12)

3. The king's ride (6:8)

5. What the king held (4:11 SKJV)

8. King Ahasuerus' wife (1:9)

Down

1. The holiday that honors Esther (9:28)

2. Esther's cousin (2:15)

4. Opposite of joy (9:22)

6. Money owed to the government (10:1 NLV)

7. Month on the Jewish calendar (3:13)

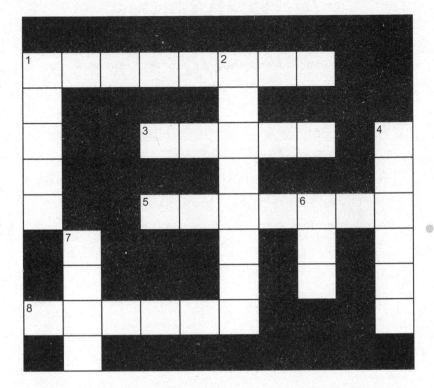

SPOTTY HEADLINE

●ONEY M●N LEAV●S ●AX
BOOT● ●O FOLLO● JESUS

Hint: One of the four Gospels is named after him.

___ ___ ___ ___ ___ ___ ___

CRAZY STRONG

And it was told to the Gazites, saying, "**Samson** has come here." And they surrounded him and <u>**lay in wait**</u> for him all **night** in the gate of the city. And they were **quiet** all night, saying, "In the **morning**, when it is day, we shall **kill** him." And Samson lay until midnight, and at **midnight** he arose and **took** the **doors** of the gate of the **city** and the two posts, <u>**bar and all**</u>, and put them on his **shoulders**, and went away with them and **carried** them up to the top of a **hill** that is before Hebron.

JUDGES 16:2–3 SKJV

SPOTTY HEADLINE

BOYS' ●OAVES A●D FIS●ES
MAKE H●GE PI●NIC

Hint: You'll eat one around noon!

___ ___ ___ ___ ___

D	F	B	S	T	L	L	I	H	T
E	T	A	R	I	M	X	Q	T	E
I	M	R	E	A	N	Y	O	R	I
R	I	A	D	W	K	O	T	N	U
R	D	N	L	N	K	I	O	I	Q
A	N	D	U	I	L	S	L	M	C
C	I	A	O	Y	M	Y	H	L	N
C	G	L	H	A	N	I	G	H	T
L	H	L	S	L	S	R	O	O	D
X	T	V	M	O	R	N	I	N	G

Jesus Heals a Blind Man

John 9:38 NLV

When Jesus healed a blind man, the Jews began hating Jesus all the more. Crack the code to find out how the blind man himself reacted.

Jesus saw a man who'd been _____ blind
(John 9:1 NLV)   34-4-8-16

"Who sinned, this man or his _____?"
(John 9:2 KJV)   36-33-6-32-13-9-5

Jesus told the man to go to the pool
of _____ (John 9:7)   31-17-19-21-10-14

The man _____ in the pool (John 9:11)   24-7-28-15-2-29

The _____ didn't believe (John 9:18)   25-20-12-35

The man's parents _____ the Jews
(John 9:22 KJV)   1-30-23-22-27-11

The Jews to the blind man: "_____ were born
in sin" (John 9:34 NLV)   18-26-3

15-32 5-33-17-29, "17 29-26 36-3-9 14-18 9-22-3-31-9

17-16 18-4-3, 19-21-8-11." 9-15-30-16 15-2 34-21-24-20-29

11-4-12-16 34-30-1-21-8-2 25-2-35-3-5 10-16-11

24-26-8-5-15-17-36-32-29 15-17-14.

CLUES:

Anything that goes against God (Romans 8:2): S ___ ___

Part of every day (Genesis 1:5): ___ ___ ___ ___ ___

Fig and olive, for example

  (Luke 21:29): T ___ ___ ___ ___

KING SOLOMON

Across

2. A curious queen's country (1 Kings 10:1)

4. What God made Solomon (1 Kings 3:12)

7. Solomon's mom (1 Kings 1:28–30)

8. Number of years Solomon reigned (1 Kings 11:42)

Down

1. Solomon's other name, given by Nathan
   (2 Samuel 12:25)

3. They turned Solomon's heart away from God
   (1 Kings 11:3)

5. He helped Solomon build the temple
   (1 Kings 5:8)

6. An expensive wood (1 Kings 10:27 NLV)

SPOTTY HEADLINE

●OW●RFUL MAN FORGIVE●
●EALOUS OLDER BR●T●ERS

Hint: His dad had given him a "coat of many colors."

___ ___ ___ ___ ___ ___

COME BEFORE WINTER

Salute **Prisca** and **Aquila** and the household of
Onesiphorus. **Erastus** remained in **Corinth**, but I have
left Trophimus sick in **Miletus**. Be **diligent** to come
before **winter**. Eubulus **greets** you, and **Pudens** and
Linus and Claudia and all the **brothers**. The Lord **Jesus
Christ** be with your spirit. **Grace** be with you. Amen.
2 TIMOTHY 4:19–22 SKJV

SCRAMBLED PLACE

TO A SUMO ARMED

Hint: Two disciples met the resurrected Jesus here.

__ __ __ __   __ __

__ __ __ __ __ __

```
E  R  A  S  T  U  S  R  G  S
T  Q  G  S  T  E  E  R  G  R
N  D  K  C  N  D  A  W  A  E
E  L  A  L  O  C  K  L  M  H
G  S  C  S  E  R  I  W  I  T
I  N  S  Q  U  U  I  S  L  O
L  E  I  H  Q  N  U  N  E  R
I  D  R  A  T  S  I  X  T  B
D  U  P  E  E  Z  K  L  U  H
B  P  R  J  C  H  R  I  S  T
```

DECODER

	1	2	3	4	5
1	W	Y	H	Q	U
2	R	X	T	V	S
3	F	G	K	M	A
4	D	P	B	I	J
5	C	E	O	L	N

PROVERBS 9:10 SKJV

23-13-52   31-52-35-21   53-31   23-13-52   54-53-21-41

44-25   23-13-52   43-52-32-44-55-55-44-55-32

53-31   11-44-25-41-53-34,   35-55-41   23-13-52

33-55-53-11-54-52-41-32-52   53-31   23-13-52   13-53-54-12

44-25   15-55-41-52-21-25-23-35-55-41-44-55-32.

ECCLESIASTES

ECCLESIASTES 12:13 SKJV

Solomon had searched everywhere for happiness,
so he had a lot to say about the meaning of life.
Crack the code to discover his final conclusion.

What the author calls himself
(Ecclesiastes 1:1)   31-34-28-32-21-15-16-8

The author had a lot of
wisdom and _____
(Ecclesiastes 1:16 SKJV)   19-13-26-30-36-35-38-29-20

There's a _____ for everything
(Ecclesiastes 3:1)   3-1-12-5

God has no _____ in fools
(Ecclesiastes 5:4 KJV)   7-14-11-25-2-17-2-4

"Eat, drink, and be _____"
(Ecclesiastes 8:15 SKJV)   23-33-18-6-39

Dead _____ smell awful (Ecclesiastes 10:1)   10-9-27-37-24

36-28-3 17-2 15-35-32-8 3-15-20 21-26-13-21-14-17-2-1-26-13

26-10 3-15-5 30-15-26-9-11 23-25-3-3-33-34:

10-37-32-2 29-26-38 25-13-38 19-28-20-31 15-27-2

21-26-12-23-32-13-38-23-5-13-3-24, 10-26-18 3-15-27-2 1-24

3-15-5 30-15-26-9-11 38-17-3-39 26-10 23-25-13.

ANGELS

Across

1. What awaits the fallen angels (Jude 6 SKJV)

4. Rulers and authorities (Colossians 1:16)

6. They might be angels (Hebrews 13:2)

7. What we shouldn't do to angels
   (Colossians 2:18 NLV)

8. What angels don't do (Matthew 22:30)

Down

2. Some angels in heaven have many of them (Revelation 4:8)

3. A type of angel (Isaiah 6:2)

5. Who sends angels to serve people? (Acts 12:11)

6. What angels sometimes carry (Numbers 22:23)

SPOTTY HEADLINE

GO● GIV●S ANIMAL ABILIT● T● TAL●!

Hint: And not just "hee haw."

___ ___ ___ ___ ___

Love Your Neighbor

Christian brother, you were **chosen** to be **free**. Be careful that you do not **please** your old selves by **sinning** because you are free. **Live** this free **life** by **loving** and **helping** others. You **obey** the whole **Law** when you do this one thing, "**Love** your **neighbor** as you love yourself."

GALATIANS 5:13–14 NLV

SPOTTY HEADLINE

●OOD NEW● OF J●SUS IS FOR A●L ●E●PLE

Hint: The word is also the name for the first four books of the New Testament.

___ ___ ___ ___ ___ ___

```
T  L  T  E  V  I  L  R  G  Z
N  O  C  W  Y  Y  E  M  N  P
A  V  R  E  M  H  P  S  I  L
I  E  B  E  T  F  I  T  V  E
T  O  L  O  F  N  R  H  O  A
S  L  R  N  N  I  P  E  L  S
I  B  A  I  X  T  L  K  E  E
R  K  N  W  C  H  O  S  E  N
H  G  N  E  I  G  H  B  O  R
C  H  E  L  P  I  N  G  X  J
```

	1	2	3	4	5
1	P	I	R	O	B
2	V	L	M	W	U
3	Z	E	J	F	D
4	X	A	T	N	Y
5	S	C	G	K	H

JOHN 14:6 NLV

33-32-51-25-51 51-42-12-35, "12 42-23 43-55-32

24-42-45 42-44-35 43-55-32 43-13-25-43-55 42-44-35

43-55-32 22-12-34-32. 44-14 14-44-32 52-42-44 53-14

43-14 43-55-32 34-42-43-55-32-13 32-41-52-32-11-43 15-45

23-32."

God's Reward for His Children

Revelation 22:20 SKJV

The book of Revelation is full of hopeful messages to God's people. Crack the code to discover Jesus' final words to His children.

John saw the new city of _____
(Revelation 21:2)
5-6-7-21-38-36-23-20-25

A constant burst of water
(Revelation 21:6 KJV)
34-33-24-27-41-16-30-18

The city had _____ gates (Revelation 21:12) 12-11-47-31-10-44

The city was laid out as a _____
(Revelation 21:16 SKJV)
39-3-29-1-35-26

The tree of life had twelve _____ of fruit
(Revelation 22:2)
42-45-32-19-14

What the prophecies contain
(Revelation 22:7 KJV)
43-28-40-13-2-8-4

Goes with Jesus' name
(Revelation 22:21 SKJV)
17-46-9-15-37-22

46-6 11-46-33 41-20-38-12-30-34-45-26-39 22-46-47-14-44

41-46-13-18-8-43 37-36-40-4, "39-29-7-47-23-40 15

17-33-25-26 3-24-30-17-42-31-40." 16-25-6-32. 26-10-20-2

37-33, 17-33-25-44, 31-33-7-19 5-26-39-29-14.

God Comes into the World

Across

2. What Jesus saves us from (Matthew 1:21)

6. What Mary laid Jesus in (Luke 2:7 KJV)

8. Who Jesus came through (Galatians 4:4)

9. Another word for Jesus' humbleness (Zechariah 9:9 KJV)

Down

1. What Mary gave birth to (Matthew 1:21)

3. Word that means "God with us" (Isaiah 7:14)

4. Jesus is like this part of a tree (Isaiah 11:1)

5. What Jesus died on (Philippians 2:8)

7. What Jesus is to the world (2 Corinthians 9:15)

DANIEL IN THE LION'S DEN

DANIEL 6:22 NLV

Daniel's enemies hated him for serving God, so they schemed to have him thrown into a den of hungry lions. Crack the code to find out what happened to Daniel!

The king wanted to set Daniel over the _____ country (Daniel 6:3)   20-7-17-36-24

A claim that someone is wrong
(Daniel 6:4 SKJV)   30-8-31-21-25-18-9-15-29-19

There wasn't _____ error or fault in
Daniel (Daniel 6:4)   14-2-34

A king's land (Daniel 6:7 KJV)   37-13-23-12-22-5-6

The king knew God could _____ Daniel
(Daniel 6:16 KJV)   10-26-39-33-32-11-28

The king's servants _____ Daniel to the
lion's den (Daniel 6:16)   27-38-16-35-1-3-4

"6-34 1-5-10 25-26-19-4 7-13-25 30-23-12-24-39 14-2-10

25-7-35-9 4-3-26 36-33-17-23-25' 6-16-21-4-7-25.

9-3-24-34 7-18-32-24 23-5-9 7-21-38-4 6-11,

27-26-8-14-35-25-24 7-11 37-2-17-20-25 4-7-18-9 13 14-6

19-16-4 12-21-33-36-4-34, 14-19-10 27-11-31-14-35-25-24

33 3-30-32-24 22-17-23-24 23-29-4-7-15-23-12

20-28-17-19-1 9-17 34-17-35, 16 37-33-19-12."

DECODER

	1	2	3	4	5
1	D	H	G	T	V
2	R	F	X	M	U
3	P	N	B	K	A
4	W	C	Y	I	S
5	J	O	Z	E	L

MATTHEW 24:44 SKJV

"14-12-54-21-54-22-52-21-54 43-52-25 35-55-45-52

33-54 21-54-35-11-43, 22-52-21 14-12-54 45-52-32 52-22

24-35-32 44-45 42-52-24-44-32-13 35-14 45-25-42-12

35-32 12-52-25-21 35-45 43-52-25 11-52 32-52-14

14-12-44-32-34."

Jesus' Golden Rule

"**Do for** other people whatever you **would like** to **have them** do for **you. This** is what the **Jewish Law** and the **early preachers said**."

MATTHEW 7:12 NLV

SPOTTY HEADLINE

JES●S-HATER BECOME● CHRISTI●N ●EADER!

Hint: His name was changed to Paul.

____ ____ ____ ____

```
R  R  J  L  J  E  W  I  S  H
P  O  W  K  M  G  Z  S  Z  V
R  F  R  H  L  E  I  J  E  W
E  O  Q  I  A  H  H  T  A  O
A  D  K  U  T  T  R  T  R  U
C  E  H  O  M  E  E  N  L  L
H  L  L  Y  H  J  K  V  Y  D
E  N  A  T  E  V  A  H  E  G
R  H  O  W  D  I  A  S  Z  R
S  G  B  Z  P  E  O  P  L  E
```

THE TEN COMMANDMENTS

EXODUS 20:2 SKJV

The Ten Commandments are the most famous rules
in human history. Crack the code to find out why
God's laws were so important for the Israelites.

"You shall not make for yourself any
graven _____" (Exodus 20:4 SKJV)   2-6-3-29-18

God will _____ those who take His name
in vain (Exodus 20:7 NLV)   16-15-30-23-20-14

Israel was to keep the Sabbath _____
 (Exodus 20:8)

9-8-11-24

God _____ the Sabbath (Exodus 20:11
KJV)   1-32-27-10-12-13-33

"You shall not covet your neighbor's _____"
(Exodus 20:17 SKJV)   28-17-21-31

There was _____ and lightning on the
mountaintop (Exodus 20:18)   19-25-22-26-7-5-4

17   3-6   19-14-31   32-8-4-33   24-8-15-4   29-8-33,   28-9-8

1-4-8-22-29-25-19   24-8-22   8-22-19   8-21   19-25-18

32-3-26-33   8-21   27-29-24-16-19,   8-22-19   8-21   19-9-13

25-8-22-20-31   8-21   1-8-30-33-3-29-5.

	1	2	3	4	5
1	K	S	T	C	X
2	Z	N	L	E	B
3	A	I	J	D	U
4	M	F	W	H	G
5	V	P	Y	R	O

PHILIPPIANS 4:4 SKJV

54-24-33-55-32-14-24 32-22 13-44-24 23-55-54-34

31-23-43-31-53-12, 31-22-34 31-45-31-32-22 32 12-31-53,

54-24-33-55-32-14-24.

ANSWER KEY

BIBLE DIAMOND PUZZLES

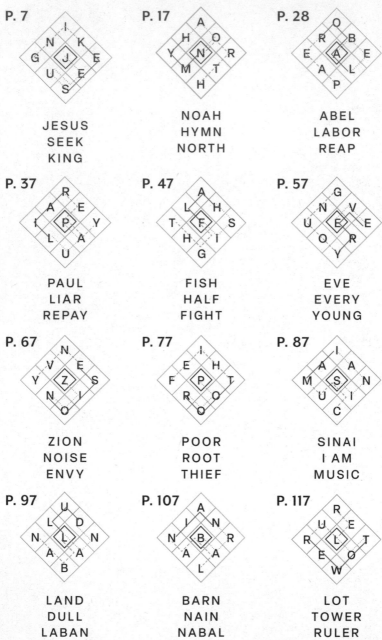

P. 7

JESUS
SEEK
KING

P. 17

NOAH
HYMN
NORTH

P. 28

ABEL
LABOR
REAP

P. 37

PAUL
LIAR
REPAY

P. 47

FISH
HALF
FIGHT

P. 57

EVE
EVERY
YOUNG

P. 67

ZION
NOISE
ENVY

P. 77

POOR
ROOT
THIEF

P. 87

SINAI
I AM
MUSIC

P. 97

LAND
DULL
LABAN

P. 107

BARN
NAIN
NABAL

P. 117

LOT
TOWER
RULER

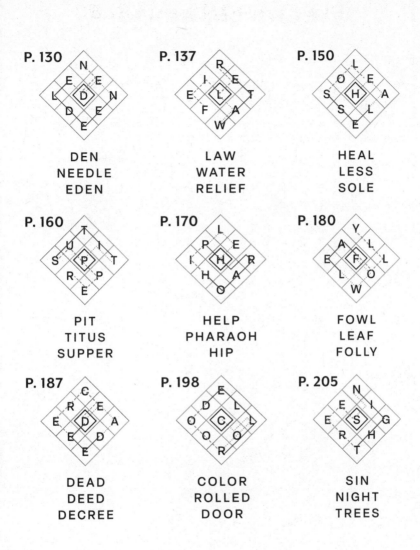

P. 130

DEN
NEEDLE
EDEN

P. 137

LAW
WATER
RELIEF

P. 150

HEAL
LESS
SOLE

P. 160

PIT
TITUS
SUPPER

P. 170

HELP
PHARAOH
HIP

P. 180

FOWL
LEAF
FOLLY

P. 187

DEAD
DEED
DECREE

P. 198

COLOR
ROLLED
DOOR

P. 205

SIN
NIGHT
TREES

WORD SEARCHES

P. 9

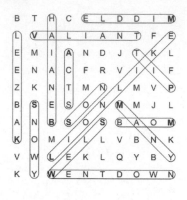

P. 15

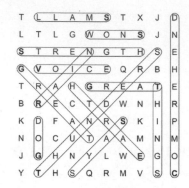

P. 21

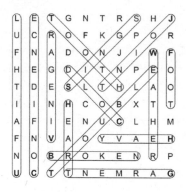

P. 27

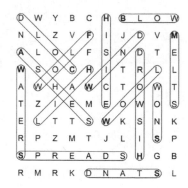

P. 33

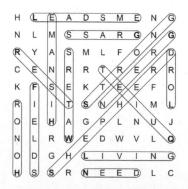

P. 39

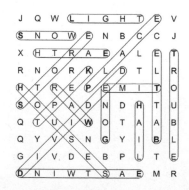

P. 45

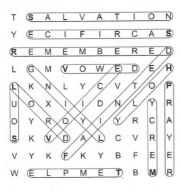

P. 49

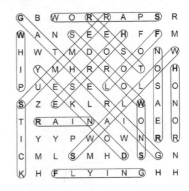

P. 55

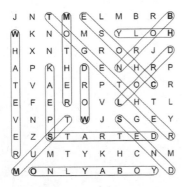

P. 59

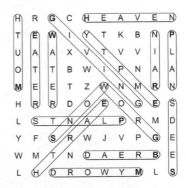

P. 65

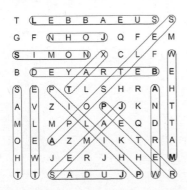

P. 69

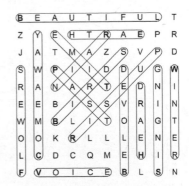

P. 75

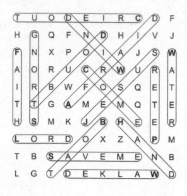

P. 79

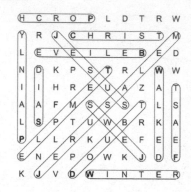

P. 85

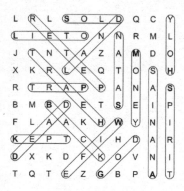

P. 89

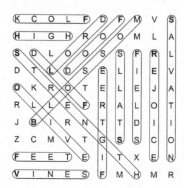

P. 95

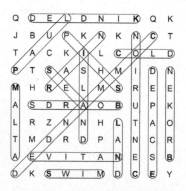

P. 99

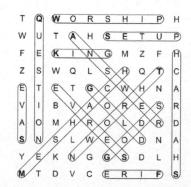

P. 105

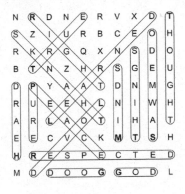

P. 109

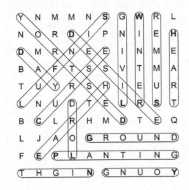

P. 115

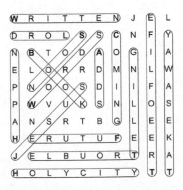

P. 119

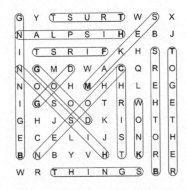

P. 125

P. 129

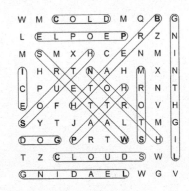

P. 135

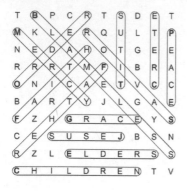

P. 139

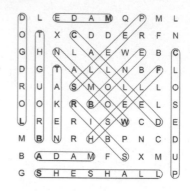

P. 145

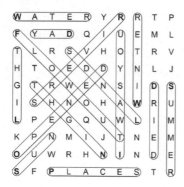

P. 149

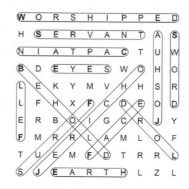

P. 155

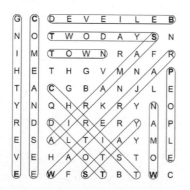

P. 159

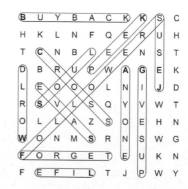

P. 165

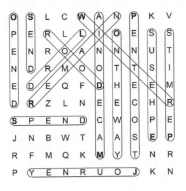

P. 169

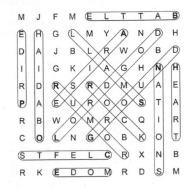

P. 175

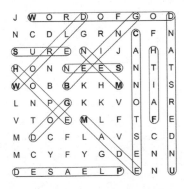

P. 179

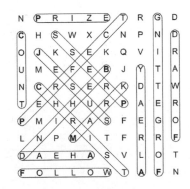

P. 185

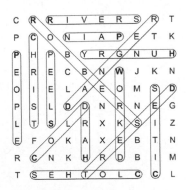

P. 191

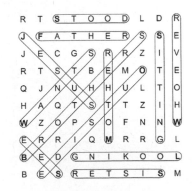

P. 197

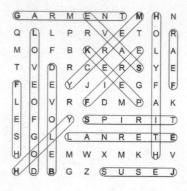

P. 203

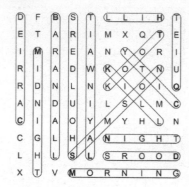

P. 209

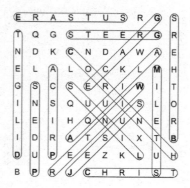

P. 215

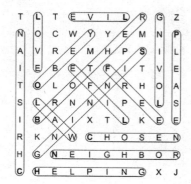

P. 223

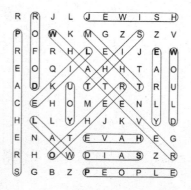

CROSSWORDS

P. 11

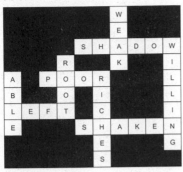

P. 19

P. 25

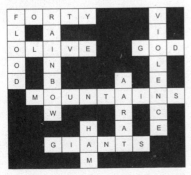

P. 31

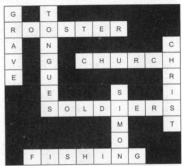

P. 41

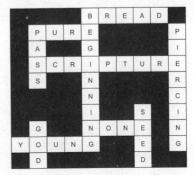

P. 53

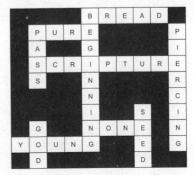

P. 63

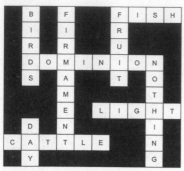

P. 73

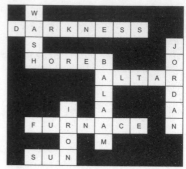

P. 83

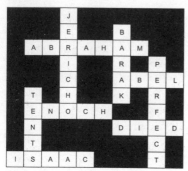

P. 93

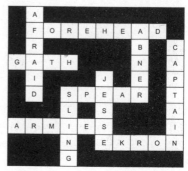

P. 103

P. 113

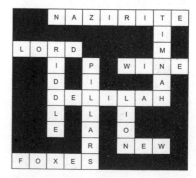

P. 121

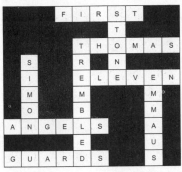

P. 127

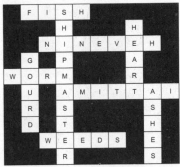

P. 133

P. 143

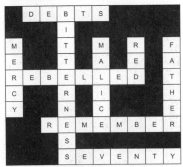

P. 147

P. 153

P. 157

P. 163

P. 167

P. 173

P. 177

P. 183

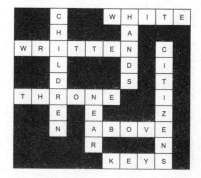

P. 189

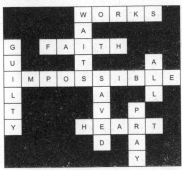

P. 195

P. 201

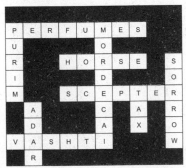

P. 207

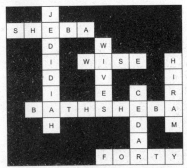

P. 213

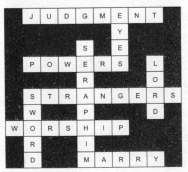

P. 219

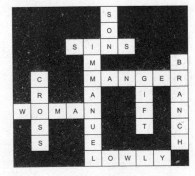

SPOTTY HEADLINES

ACROSTICS

P. 12

Jonah / sailors / stopped / forty / booth / sun / forsake

Then the Lord spoke to the fish, and it spit Jonah out onto the dry land.

P. 16

Philistines / servants / sheep / followed / armor / gods / sword

So David won the fight against the Philistine with a sling and a stone.

P. 22

away / thousand / Peter / strong / Jesus / faith / doubt

Those in the boat worshiped Jesus. They said, "For sure, You are the Son of God!"

P. 29

Pharaoh / Egyptians / gave / followed / out

Thus the Lord saved Israel that day out of the hand of the Egyptians, and Israel saw the Egyptians dead on the seashore.

P. 34

Ahab / Carmel / spoken / swords / stones / bull / sacrifice

Then the fire of the LORD fell and consumed the burnt sacrifice and the wood and the stones and the dust, and licked up the water that was in the trench.

P. 36

Balak / hinder / donkey / thrust / sword / promote

And the LORD put a word in Balaam's mouth and said, "Return to Balak, and thus you shall speak."

P. 42

Bethlehem / Moabitess / why / fall / gleaned / covers / Jesse

And the women, her neighbors, gave it a name, saying, "There is a son born to Naomi," and they called his name Obed. He is the father of Jesse, the father of David.

P. 50

Cyprus / centurion / Havens / swim / Malta / hand

And Paul dwelled two whole years in his own hired house, and received all who came to him.

P. 56

Jericho / trumpets / dawning / flat / spy

So the LORD was with Joshua, and his fame was reported throughout all the country.

P. 61

Mordecai / Esther / scepter / wicked / family / ring

So they hanged Haman on the gallows that he had prepared for Mordecai. Then the king's anger was pacified.

P. 70

woman / sought / carcass / riddle / Philistines / weak / offer

And Samson took hold of the two middle pillars on which the house stood, and on which it was held up, of the one with his right hand and of the other with his left.

P. 76

Galilee / disciples / mother / servants / jars / purifying / brim

This beginning of miracles Jesus did in Cana of Galilee and revealed His glory. And His disciples believed in Him.

P. 86

Magdalene / sepulchre / white / Didymus / finger / know

This is the disciple who testifies of these things, and wrote these things, and we know that his testimony is true.

P. 91

magicians / frogs / away / children / brought / passover

Then Pharaoh called for Moses and Aaron at night. He said, "Get up and go away from my people, both you and the people of Israel. Go and worship the Lord, as you have said."

P. 100

cubits / provinces / golden / fiery / Meshach / king / midst

Then the king promoted Shadrach, Meshach, and Abed-nego in the province of Babylon.

P. 106

Pentecost / tongues / Libya / new / saved / Nazareth / miracles

Then those who gladly received his word were baptized, and the same day about three thousand souls were added to them.

P. 116

waters / shadow / prepare / enemies / oil / days

The LORD is my shepherd. I shall not want.

P. 123

Abraham / love / mountains / donkey / offering / wood

And He said, "Do not lay your hand on the boy or do anything to him, for now I know that you fear God, seeing you have not withheld your son, your only son, from Me."

P. 131

child / ministered / word / servant / morning / you

Samuel grew. And the Lord was with him and made everything he said come true.

P. 140

prophet / wholeheartedly / sundial / middle / grave / father

"The Lord will save me. And we will sing my songs with harps all the days of our life in the house of the Lord."

P. 151

Israel / prayer / Christ / live / whom / beautiful / disobedient

For everyone who calls on the name of the Lord will be saved from the punishment of sin.

P. 161

fasted / should / mind / you / within

So the wall was finished on the twenty-fifth day of the month of Elul, in fifty-two days.

P. 171

whirlwind / foundations / prey / judgment / covenant / burns

And the LORD turned the captivity of Job when he prayed for his friends. Also the LORD gave Job twice as much as he had before.

P. 186

wisdom / Tyre / seashore / porch / fulfilled / gold / navy

For it came to pass, when Solomon was old, that his wives turned away his heart after other gods. And his heart was not perfect with the LORD his God, as was the heart of his father, David.

P. 193

Midianites / valor / Egypt / dew / hundred / bowed

And the three hundred blew the trumpets, and the LORD set every man's sword against one another throughout all the army.

P. 204

born / parents / Siloam / washed / Jews / feared / you

He said, "I do put my trust in You, Lord." Then he bowed down before Jesus and worshiped Him.

P. 211

Preacher / knowledge / time / pleasure / merry / flies

Let us hear the conclusion of the whole matter: Fear God and keep His commandments, for this is the whole duty of man.

P. 217

Jerusalem / fountain / twelve / square / kinds / sayings / Christ

He who testifies these things says, "Surely I come quickly." Amen. Even so, come, Lord Jesus.

P. 220

whole / accusation / any / kingdom / deliver / brought

"My God sent His angel and shut the lions' mouths. They have not hurt me, because He knows that I am not guilty, and because I have done nothing wrong to you, O king."

P. 224

image / punish / holy / blessed / wife / thunder

I am the Lord your God, who brought you out of the land of Egypt, out of the house of bondage.

DECODERS

P. 13

And God saw everything that He had made, and behold, it was very good. And the evening and the morning were the sixth day.

P. 23

For with the heart man believes to righteousness, and with the mouth confession is made to salvation.

P. 35

So then, brothers, we are children not of the bondwoman but of the free.

P. 43

"For God so loved the world that He gave His only begotten Son, that whoever believes in Him should not perish but have everlasting life."

P. 46

And let the peace of God rule in your hearts, to which you also are called in one body. And be thankful.

P. 51

The fear of the Lord is the beginning of knowledge, but fools despise wisdom and instruction.

P. 60

"Do not make for yourselves a god to look like anything that is in heaven above or on the earth below or in the waters under the earth."

P. 66

There is a season for everything and a time for every purpose under heaven.

P. 71

Peter said to them, "Be sorry for your sins and turn from them and be baptized in the name of Jesus Christ, and your sins will be forgiven. You will receive the gift of the Holy Spirit."

P. 80
And I, John, saw the holy city, new Jerusalem, coming down out of heaven from God, prepared as a bride adorned for her husband.

P. 81
In the beginning God created the heaven and the earth.

P. 90
I may be able to speak the languages of men and even of angels, but if I do not have love, it will sound like noisy brass.

P. 96
Now faith is the substance of things hoped for, the evidence of things not seen.

P. 101
He who does not love does not know God, for God is love.

P. 110
There is one Lord and one faith and one baptism.

P. 111
"For I know the plans I have for you," says the Lord, "plans for well-being and not for trouble, to give you a future and a hope."

P. 122
"Have I not commanded you? Be strong and of good courage. Do not be afraid or be dismayed, for the Lord your God is with you wherever you go."

P. 136
Your Word is a lamp to my feet and a light to my path.

P. 141
Blessed are those who hunger and thirst after righteousness, for they shall be filled.

P. 181

Therefore if any man is in Christ, he is a new creature. Old things have passed away; behold, all things have become new.

P. 192

"Where were you when I laid the foundations of the earth? Declare, if you have understanding."

P. 199

The Lord is my Shepherd. I will have everything I need.

P. 210

The fear of the Lord is the beginning of wisdom, and the knowledge of the holy is understanding.

P. 216

Jesus said, "I am the Way and the Truth and the Life. No one can go to the Father except by Me."

P. 221

"Therefore you also be ready, for the Son of Man is coming at such an hour as you do not think."

P. 225

Rejoice in the Lord always, and again I say, rejoice.

SCRAMBLES

MORE GREAT BIBLE FUN FOR KIDS!

Here's a fun and fascinating book offering 20, 6 question quizzes for 6–10-year-olds. Each quiz starts easy, with questions from the most familiar stories, then gets progressively harder. If you get stuck, "Bible Bonuses" provide help, and each question is accompanied by an intriguing "Did You Know?" that adds to the fun.

Paperback / ISBN 978-1-63609-360-4